CONFRONTING
CURRICULUM
REFORM

CONTRIBUTING AUTHORS

ELLIOT W. EISNER
Stanford University

BENJAMIN S. BLOOM
University of Chicago

LEE J. CRONBACH
Stanford University

ROBERT KARPLUS
University of California, Berkeley

ROBERT G. BRIDGHAM
Stanford University

EDWARD G. BEGLE
Stanford University

MICHAEL SCRIVEN
University of California, Berkeley

IRVING KAUFMAN
The City University of New York

EDMUND BURKE FELDMAN
University of Georgia

JAMES B. MACDONALD
University of Wisconsin, Milwaukee

RICHARD E. SCHUTZ
Southwest Regional Laboratory

ROBERT G. HANVEY
Indiana University

JAN L. TUCKER
Stanford University

MERLIN C. WITTROCK
University of California, Los Angeles

CONFRONTING CURRICULUM REFORM

EDITED BY ELLIOT W. EISNER

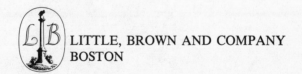

LITTLE, BROWN AND COMPANY
BOSTON

PREFACE

The relationship of scientific theory to practice in the field of curriculum is, as in other fields in education, a tenuous one at best. Educational phenomena are much more complicated than the best theoretical networks we have and more often than not escape the nets that curriculum theorists have woven. This state of affairs in part emanates from the general usefulness of social science theory to educational problems. Theories that are developed in non-educational settings are applied to educational practice in the hope that they will predict and control educational phenomena. In addition, theories derived from laboratories using rigorous controls find their way into settings that have no such controls, settings in which the unpredictable, the random, the contingent are the rule rather than the exception. In my opinion, these two conditions — the fact that social science theory is often applied to education after having been developed to deal with other phenomena, and the fact that such theory is frequently developed in settings in which the systematic control of stimuli is possible — account for the feckless character of theory in educational practice. But there is another reason as well. The theory that has been developed in the field of curriculum has not developed from the study of curricular practices. Concepts and principles have been advocated that have grown out of a rational analysis of what people developing curricula *ought* to do. Whether these prescriptions do in fact square with practice and whether they can improve practice remains to be seen since the number of empirical studies which describe and analyze the relationship between principle and practice in curriculum is exceedingly small.

This book represents an effort to find out, from those who have struggled with the tasks of curriculum making and curriculum implementation, how they have gone about their work. In it we attempt to look into the problems that are indigenous to curriculum making, to identify their common and unique characteristics, and to suggest alternative approaches to curriculum development from those generally used since the middle 1950s.

The people who have prepared the articles that constitute this book are eminently qualified for their task. Each has competence and insight into educational practice. But more, each has directed or participated directly in the development of curricula. Collectively they have been responsible for the management of millions of dollars in the pursuit of improved curriculum making. We have here, then, a group of individuals who know curriculum making from first-hand experience with the task. It is from these individuals and from the practices of curriculum development, curriculum implementation, and curriculum evaluation that the field of curriculum might build its empirical foundations.

These articles were originally prepared for presentation at the Cubberley Curriculum Conference held at Stanford University in May, 1969. As director of that conference, I am in debt to Dean Tom James and the faculty of the School of Education, who recognized the importance and timeliness of bringing curriculum theorists and curriculum project directors together to discuss problems peculiar to the field of curriculum. I am especially indebted to the members of the Conference Committee, professors Edward Begle, Robert Bridgham, William Iverson, and Jan Tucker, for providing good counsel and for sharing the tasks of putting together an educational conference. I also wish to thank Decker Walker, who, at the time, was a doctoral student in General Curriculum at Stanford, for his invaluable assistance in handling so many of the details of the conference. Finally, I am in deepest debt to those whose words fill these pages. Those who know the field of education in this country know their work and must, therefore, appreciate their willingness to leave it in order to come to Stanford to share with the rest of us the insights that work has provided.

ELLIOT W. EISNER

CONTENTS

CONFRONTING CURRICULUM REFORM

INTRODUCTION

ELLIOT W. EISNER

CURRICULUM DEVELOPMENT: SOURCES FOR A FOUNDATION FOR THE FIELD OF CURRICULUM

To any student of American education the emergence of the "new curricula" has been one of the hallmarks of educational change since 1955. Although historians will undoubtedly describe this period in American education as one in which the computer entered the classroom, programmed instruction made its formal debut, and the civil rights movement and the black revolution began to challenge the accepted content and goals of American schools, surely the development and implementation of new curricula, not only in the sciences and in mathematics but in the social sciences and in the arts, will be identified as one, if not the major development during the period. The alphabets are now familiar — BSCS, SMSG, AAAS, PSSC — each representing millions of dollars of expenditures for the improvement of educational programs. Harvard Project Physics, MAN: A Course of Study, The Elementary School Science Program, and CEMREL's Aesthetic Education Program, like the projects previously mentioned, have all been formulated and developed since 1957. Indeed, a project such as SMSG has expanded so rapidly that about half of the high school students studying mathematics are now using the "new math." My thesis is that these projects are important not only in their own right, but also because they provide the necessary conditions for building the empirical foundations of the field of curriculum.

One need not extensively recount the conditions that gave rise to the new curricula to understand that they were developed in large measure in response to a deeply felt social-political crisis. The state of the curriculum in American schools, at least as perceived by critics of progressivism, and the second-best efforts of the United States to send a space module around this planet, were grounds enough to attempt to revamp the curriculum. The problem as it was conceived, at least in part, was to make the school's program, its curriculum, more intellectually respectable by developing subject-matter curricula that more accurately represented the values, methods, and content of the academic disciplines. The laxity of the school (fancied or real), especially the American high school, needed to be overcome by giving scholars from the disciplines access to curriculum decision-making. Schools that *purportedly* catered to the student's interests, that *purportedly* emphasized his whole reactions to educational events, etc., needed now — especially in view of the political situation of the late fifties — to attend to the student's intellectual development. Backed by both prestige and funds from the National Science Foundation and from the United States Office of Education (it is estimated that well over 100 million dollars have been allocated for curriculum development in science and mathematics over the past ten-year period), leaders of the new movement had access to the schools. This movement, which is said to have started in 1952 with Max Beberman's work in mathematics at the University of Illinois, now has grown to the point where in the social sciences alone over fifty projects are listed. A large one such as MAN: A Course of Study operates on a budget of about 3 million dollars per year and utilizes the efforts of at least one educational laboratory to implement its work.

These developments in the field of curriculum were the motivating force for the Cubberley Curriculum Conference at Stanford University in May, 1969. Because so much was going on, it was believed important to bring some of the leaders of the movement together to get a view — first-hand — of what they were up to. How were they proceeding with their work? What problems were they encountering? How were they coping with these problems? Were they evaluating the programs they were building and, if so, how? What did they see as the future of curriculum development in their own field? These questions animated those of us at

Stanford who gave direction to the conference, and because at least one major project, SMSG, was being directed by one of our own colleagues we decided, sans federal funding, to call together a group who could perhaps begin to answer the questions that nagged us.

But because we wanted more than a mere recounting of the past, we decided to invite the most perceptive individuals we could find to comment on the papers that were presented at the conference. These commentators were asked to appraise critically what had been presented, and all except one had access to the papers prior to their presentation.

Only an individual with tunnel vision would subscribe to the belief that the best way to construct an educational program for a school is to develop individual subject-matter curricula unrelated to a general curriculum plan and then allow prestige or publicity to determine which of these are implemented. Such an ad hoc approach has certain similarities to unplanned urban development: after a few years we are forced to live with the consequences of short-sighted, short-term decision-making. To look at the overall implications of the new curriculum, three curriculum generalists were asked to present papers which, it was hoped, would raise important issues or question the assumptions upon which present programs are built and perhaps help American education avoid the possible disasters of curriculum reform by crisis. We wanted to identify the problems and tasks confronting the curriculum maker in any field. Were there some common tasks and procedures in curriculum development? Were some types of problems unique and, if so, did their uniqueness stem from the nature of the particular subject matter, from the way in which the curriculum staff was organized, or from some other source? By bringing curriculum makers together with curriculum generalists we hoped to be able to identify some of the common and unique aspects of the curriculum development process.

That these questions have not been previously raised is due, at least in part, to the way in which the new curriculum projects have been formed and operated. More often than not they have been developed first at the secondary level and then have crept slowly downward to the junior high school and elementary school. They have, in almost all cases, been developed on an independent basis; that is, they have been developed within a particular field

of study and for schools in general rather than for particular
schools. This method of curriculum building has failed to relate
new curricula in various fields or to consider the effect of one
new curriculum on existing programs.

In addition to these characteristics a substantial proportion of
the new curricula has shared a common set of assumptions: the
content of the curriculum should be drawn from the major academic disciplines. Until quite recently no one challenged the goal
of teaching students the concepts and procedures of chemistry,
anthropology, or mathematics.[1] Sputnik, it seems, was proof
enough that the intellectual rigor (and vigor?) of the academic
disciplines needed to be injected into programs purportedly concerned with the development of the whole child. How could learning to think like a scientist be bad?[2]

Another characteristic of the curriculum reform movement is
a spin-off of its isolation from other aspects of the school's program. Virtually all of the new curricula have been designed to
fit into, rather than to challenge or to alter the existing organizational structure of the schools. If one is developing a curriculum
in one part of the country which is funded on a large-scale basis
for general implementation, it is reasonable to avoid developing
programs that require a radical overhaul of American public
schools. The likelihood of implementing programs that make
drastic demands upon the structure of the school is small. It is
reasonable, therefore, at least from the standpoint of curriculum
specialists working in subject-matter areas, to focus on the problem of building a program that can be plugged in almost anywhere. For maximum implementation one needs a program that
is adaptable. Such an approach has, of course, a great virtue: it
increases the likelihood that it will be made available to students.
No medicine can have any effect without contacting the organism.
The vice of this approach is that it does not look far enough into
the cause of the disease, if disease there is. If the maladies from
which American education is suffering reside in the basic assumptions it makes about what role students should play, about how
content, method, and aims should be determined, about how educational growth should be assessed, about what relationship
schools should have to the social and political world in which
they function, then the treatment of symptoms — even when
lauded by *Time* and *Life* — might in the long run be a setback

to educational progress. What looks like salvation in the early sixties might turn out to be treatment for the wrong disease by the end of the decade.

These characteristics of the curriculum reform movement made the need for curriculum generalists apparent. The need to develop or suggest relationships among fields has become acute during the past fifteen years. In addition, we wanted to find out, as candidly as possible, how things were going. What, if any, were the real bugs in curriculum making, the type of difficulties that did not get into the literature. Through dialogue in a comfortable and intimate environment, we hoped to exchange candid observations, for surely they are not now in the educational literature. How curricula are developed and implemented is an unstudied problem in American education. With the exception of four studies,[3] two of them anecdotal, no attempt has been made, as far as I know, to study systematically the way in which curricula are actually made by curriculum development groups. Why this is the case, at least from the standpoint of the curriculum maker, is clear. Those who see their task as developing new curricula are not inclined to divert funds, personnel and energy to the task of studying how that task is pursued. Yet the study of how that task is pursued is, as I have indicated elsewhere,[4] one of the primary boulders from which the building blocks of the field of curriculum can be cut.

It has long been apparent that while the field of curriculum has a long line of educational scholars who have contributed mightily to the conceptual aspects of the field — e.g., Franklin Bobbitt, William Kilpatrick, Henry Harap, W. W. Charters, Henry Morrison, Ralph W. Tyler, Hilda Taba, B. O. Smith, John I. Goodlad[5] — its empirical aspect, that is, the study of processes central to curriculum as a field of study, has been neglected. When one stops to realize that the recommended procedures for building educational programs have been based upon little or no actual study of the process of curriculum development one cannot help wondering about the validity of such recommendations. Thus, it is apparent that while the conceptual handles that have been advanced so admirably by Tyler, Goodlad, and others are necessary for conducting inquiry into curriculum problems, without empirical test they lack the grounding necessary for building the field as an area of scholarly study and artful practice.

Take, for example, Ralph Tyler's curriculum rationale cited above. It raises questions that could profitably be asked about curriculum development projects now being implemented. How are objectives stated? How are they developed? What relation do they bear to the experiences the students are supposed to have? Tyler's rationale also suggests questions about continuity, sequence, and integration, as well as the uses of evaluation and the relationship of evaluation techniques to program objectives. In short, conceptual schemes like Tyler's provide an analytic tool for comparing and contrasting curricula as finished products, enabling the evaluator to determine their strengths and weaknesses.

The curriculum reform movement not only provides the products capable of being studied in their finished form, it provides an excellent opportunity to study the process of curriculum development. As I have already indicated, this is an unstudied area in American education. How in fact do curricula get built? Who makes what decisions? To what extent is psychological theory used in making curriculum decisions? How is feedback secured? What roles do teachers play in the process? Are general social concerns used to determine what shall be taught and how? How are teachers instructed in the use of new curricula? What role does evaluation perform in curriculum making and when in the life of a project does it enter the scene? What generalizations, if any, can be securely made about the processes of curriculum building and what principles are useful in organizing the work?

These and other questions can be asked by curriculum researchers or developers. If generalizations are forthcoming, the field might be in a position to help new curriculum development groups avoid the pitfalls encountered by the old. Some of the useful research will probably be hard-headed studies approximating experimental paradigms; others will be a type of clinical empiricism that is closer to anthropological methods of observation and to the canons of art criticism than to the laboratory. In either case, the emergence of the curriculum reform movement and the array of projects it has spawned provide a potentially productive source of subject matter upon which the empirical foundations of the curriculum field may be built.

Although study of the processes of curriculum development is an area of glaring neglect in the field, it is not the only area that needs attention. Once curricula are developed they need to be implemented in schools in ways that will violate neither the integrity of the people who are to use them nor the aims to which they are directed. This is no mean task. If one thing has been learned during the past fifteen years, it is that the so-called ideal of "teacher-proof" curriculum is a mirage subscribed to by those who have little contact with the subtleties of the classroom. The task of appropriately implementing a curriculum which has cost millions to develop is one that is literally vital. New curricula often demand of teachers a new way of looking at the task of instruction. They often require that teachers deal with concepts and procedures as new to them as to the students. To perform effectively the assignments outlined in curriculum guides, to work with content in a way that does not violate its integrity and at the same time to maintain the ecology of the classroom is indeed a complicated task. Errors in the use of a new curriculum can be both those of omission and commission. The former ensue from inadequate study of the material by the teacher; the latter errors emanate from a misunderstanding of what the material is intended for. Didactic teaching of inquiry-oriented curricula is not uncommon. Nor is it rare to attempt to implement a curriculum aimed at the development of critical thinking in a school whose organizational pattern and system of sanctions contradict the very goals espoused by the program it adopts.[6] To expect to develop the student's abilities to initiate his own learning and become responsible for his own education and, at the same time, require that he carry a hall pass and show it to each hall guard on his trip to the washroom is to breed a type of contradiction (some would call it hypocrisy) that typifies too many American schools.

What is to be done about such conditions? How does one go about implementing a curriculum in a school? What role can teachers and students play in this process? What type of support, if any, is needed from the community? How can the organizational climate of the school[7] be altered to support a curriculum whose aims deviate from those now being used? The study and development of methods of curriculum implementation is a second source for building an empirical foundation for the field of curriculum.

Because many of the new curricula are intended to develop competencies that go well beyond the traditional goals of school programs, the need for developing sensitive and imaginative approaches to evaluation is especially acute. Curriculum experts gen-

erally agree on what evaluation should accomplish. It should help
determine whether objectives have been attained, help diagnose
learning difficulties, and provide a picture of a student's progress
before the end of the term. But knowing the goals of evaluation
and achieving them are two different things. From my vantage
point, instruments and procedures that actually function in the
ways described are prominent by their scarcity. The conceptual
work by Scriven, Stake, Cronbach, Stuffelbeam and others are
significant advances in broadening the conception of evaluation.[8]
A broader, more comprehensive view might, in the long run, provide more effective means of building curriculum and facilitating
instruction. At present, however, the tools to assess process, for
example, are limited. Most curriculum developers take their evaluative cues from the subtle and not so subtle events in the classroom. They attempt to make sense of a wide array of events they
confront in process: informal feedback from teachers, responses
from students, reports from administrators, observations of the
staff. Are such data sloppy? Are such methods unreliable? By
hard-headed standards they probably are, but such methods often
tend to have greater validity than many of the insensitive instruments now available which purportedly assess "achievement."

The development of new curricula also makes possible the development of evaluation procedures capable of locating both the
source of difficulties and the strengths in the curricula that have
been developed. For example, the lack of achievement on the
part of students using a new curriculum may emanate from a
variety of sources: the material might not be clear to the teachers
that are to use it, the learning activities that have been suggested
by the curriculum makers might be too difficult or uninteresting
to students, the instructional devices that are designed to "carry"
the concepts and generalizations might not actually do so. The
importance of identifying the source or sources of curriculum difficulties is apparent to anyone who has attempted to build and
improve such programs. For years evaluation has implied the
analysis and appraisal of student behavior in relation to curriculum
objectives. With the new curricula it has become apparent that
the content of the curriculum as well as its mode of organization
needs to be evaluated to determine *why* the curriculum has succeeded or *why* it has failed to facilitate the educational development of the student. Indeed, it has become apparent that we

must go beyond evaluating the behavior of the student, we must even go beyond evaluating the content of the programs; we must also appraise the art of instruction. Poor instruction can scuttle a good curriculum and artful instruction may be an empty enterprise without content worth the student's time. The advent of the new curricula has laid the groundwork for the development of evaluation procedures and concepts which may also contribute to the construction of the empirical foundation of curriculum as a field of study.

One potential source for developing the foundations of the curriculum field will be the establishing of appropriate roles for specialists in constructing new curricula. As both Judd and Bobbitt realized fifty years ago and as Herrick and Tyler re-emphasized twenty years ago, the task of curriculum development is one that demands a wide variety of competencies.[9] Curriculum building is not a one-man job. But like observations concerning evaluation, it is one thing to state that subject-matter specialists, psychologists, and philosophers should be consulted in curriculum development and it is quite another to identify the appropriate types of questions to ask them. And, having obtained answers to those questions, how are those answers to be related to one another in the act of curriculum building? Thus far, little in the literature suggests how such specialists are to be used or how the contributions of their fields are to be employed in curriculum-making. As curriculum development projects learn to use specialists effectively, we might then begin to identify more helpful ways for guiding curriculum makers in the use of specialized academics.

Another potential contribution of the curriculum reform movement to the field of curriculum is an indirect consequence of the way in which curriculum development has been approached. As I have already indicated, curricula have been developed primarily on a subject-matter basis, a basis close to the academic disciplines from which the fields are drawn. As Bloom has indicated,[10] this mode of development is perhaps more closely allied to the background and convenience of the teacher than it is to the needs or interests of the student. The emphasis on the academic discipline and on discipline-generated problems in contrast to problems generated from the interests of the student as person and as citizen is now being brought into question as students are becoming more vocal and less willing to accept the educational prescriptions of academics and school-board members a generation or more older than they.

The possibility of developing curricula which cut across fields, curricula which focus upon the persistent and literally vital questions of our time — over-population, pollution of our natural resources, relations between the nations and the races, between the generations, and between the rich and the poor — offers promising educational counterparts to present programs that appear to touch the lives of only a small proportion of students at best. While the treatment of such problems will of course require that theory, data, and method from the academic disciplines be used, such problems will require that teachers from a variety of fields work together to illuminate the multi-faceted aspects of all large-scale social or economic problems. In short, the almost exclusive emphasis upon discipline-based curricula has begun to bring into question one of the major assumptions underlying such curricula. The failure of the most heavily funded projects to develop alternative curriculum schemes has begun to provide the impetus for the development of other approaches to curriculum building.[11]

A final contribution that the curriculum reform movement can make to the field of curriculum is to study the way in which the instructional support system and the organizational structure of the school affect the potency of its new programs.

As I have already indicated, new curricula frequently demand of teachers that they look at subject matter in new ways and that they modify radically their own modes of instruction. But not only must these "in-class" changes be brought about; in many cases the culture of the school must be altered if the goals of new projects are to be realized. Edward T. Hall, Robert Dreeben, Fred Newmann and Donald Oliver have revealed with great insight how the muted cues of culture and the organizational patterns of schooling affect students in school.[12] Philip W. Jackson's extremely sensitive analysis of life in classrooms has brought home the impact of institutional life on the elementary school child.[13] We have begun to recognize that not only the curriculum as a whole needs attention but that the cultural press of the school — its implicit curriculum — needs to be attended to intelligently if the programs that are employed are to have effect. This area especially has been neglected in the curriculum reform movement. Curriculum developers appear to have worked on the assumption that programs can be installed in much the same way that a new muffler is installed in an old car. Such an assumption is of course fallacious. Adjustments that both students and teachers make to programs brought into a school are often sufficiently adaptive to maintain the program with little or no important change. What must be done to alter the instructional system and organizational structure of a school so that it encourages the educationally valuable is the question in point. Curriculum research can now deal descriptively with the problems of how students and teacher adapt to new curricula. And with the cooperation of school personnel, experimental studies can be planned to determine, for example, if alteration of the reward system of the school can increase teachers' and students' willingness to take intellectual and emotional risks with the new curricula.

Although the curriculum reform movement started as an effort to meet a social-political crisis by overhauling the curriculum of the American school, the contribution it might eventually make to American education may go well beyond the improvement of subject-matter curricula. The curriculum reform movement, I have argued, provides the necessary conditions for developing the foundations of the field of curriculum. The processes of curriculum development, of curriculum implementation, and of curriculum evaluation provide natural laboratories to help specialists in the field of curriculum understand how curriculum decision-making can be improved. The conceptual insights coming from such study might require that cherished notions in the field be abandoned for those more empirically adequate. It might also provide the empirical grounds for substantiating the validity of the concepts now employed. In any case, it is clear that students of curriculum have an unparalleled opportunity to study phenomena that are truly indigenous to the field of education. The papers which follow are intended to represent an opening foray into that field.

REFERENCES

[1] Mark Krug, "Bruner's New Social Studies: A Critique," *Social Education,* Vol. XXX, No. 6, October 1966; Herbert Kliebard, "Structure of the Disciplines as an Educational Slogan," *Teachers College Record,* Vol. 66, No. 7, April 1965; Fred M. Newmann, "Questioning the Place of Social Science Disciplines in Education," *Teachers College Record,* Vol. 69, No. 1, October 1967.

2 The most prominent and influential statement of this view is, of course, Jerome Bruner's *The Process of Education*, Cambridge: Harvard University Press, 1961.

3 Robert McClure, "Procedures, Processes, and Products in Curriculum Development," unpublished Ed. D. dissertation, University of California, Los Angeles, 1965; Decker Walker, *A Case Study of the Process of Curriculum Development*, Stanford University, School of Education; Paul Hurd, *Biological Education in America Secondary Schools 1890-1960*, Washington: American Institute of Biological Sciences, 1961; William Wooton, *S.M.S.G.*, *The Making of a Curriculum*, New Haven and London: Yale University Press, 1965.

4 Elliot W. Eisner, "Curriculum Theory and the Concept of Educational Milieu," *High School Journal*, Vol. LI, No. 3, December 1967.

5 Franklin Bobbitt, *The Curriculum*, Boston: Houghton, Mifflin Co., 1918; William H. Kilpatrick, *The Project Method: The Use of the Purposeful Act in the Educative Process*, New York: Teachers College, 1925; Henry Harap, *The Technique of Curriculum Making*, New York: The Macmillian Co., 1928; W. W. Charters, *Curriculum Construction*, New York: The Macmillan Co., 1923; Henry C. Morrison, *The Curriculum of the Common School*, Chicago: University of Chicago Press, 1940; Ralph W. Tyler, *Basic Principles of Curriculum and Instruction: Syllabus for Education 360*, Chicago: University of Chicago Press, 1950; Hilda Taba, *Curriculum Development; Theory and Practice*, New York: Harcourt, Brace and World, 1962; B. O. Smith, "Dimensions of Curriculum," mimeo, 14 pp., 1967; John I. Goodlad, "The School Scene in Review," *The School Review*, Vol. LXVI, No. 4, Winter 1958.

6 Philip W. Jackson, *Life in Classrooms*, New York: Holt, Rinehart and Winston, 1968; Robert Dreeben, *On What Is Learned in School*, Reading: Addison-Wesley Publishing Co., 1968.

7 For an imaginative and useful approach to the assessment of the organizational climate of the school see Andrew Halpin and Don Croft, *The Organizational Climate of the School*, Washington: U. S. Office of Education, 1962.

8 Michael Scriven, "The Methodology of Evaluation," *AERA Monograph on Curriculum Evaluation*, No. 1, Chicago: Rand McNally & Co., 1968; Robert Stake, "The Countenance of Educational Evaluation," *Teachers College Record*, Vol. 68, No. 7, April 1967; Lee J. Cronbach, "Course Improvement Through Evaluation," *Teachers College Record*, Vol. 64, No. 8, May 1963; Daniel Stuffelbeam, "The Use and Abuse of Evaluation in Title III," *Theory into Practice*, Vol. VI, No. 3, June 1967.

9 Charles Judd, "The Scientific Technique of Curriculum-Making," *School and Society*, Vol. XV, No. 367, January 1922; Franklin Bobbitt, *How to Make a Curriculum*, New York: Houghton Mifflin Co., 1924; Virgil Herrick and Ralph W. Tyler, "Next Steps in the Development of a More Adequate Curriculum Theory," *Toward Improved Curriculum Theory* (Supplementary Educational Monograph, No. 71), Chicago: University of Chicago Press, 1950.

10 See Professor Bloom's summary statement at the end of this volume.

[11] For an excellent example of an effort to restructure the catagories used to define educational programs, the reader is referred to the imaginative program at St. Mary's High School in Chicago. In that school courses have been radically altered to better suit the interests of the students the school serves.

[12] Edward T. Hall, *The Silent Language,* Garden City: Doubleday, 1959; Robert Dreeben, *op. cit.*; Fred Newmann and Donald Oliver, "Education and Community," *Harvard Educational Review,* Vol. 37, No. 1, Winter 1967.

[13] Philip W. Jackson, *op. cit.*

PART ONE

THE CONFERENCE

of one year performed at about the same level as the
of another year. Nor does it matter that the A students
ol do about as well as the F students of another school.
ecome "conditioned" to the normal distribution, we
olicies in these terms and are horrified when some
mpts to recommend a very different distribution of
even more important, we find ways of convincing
t they can only do C work or D work by our grading
even by our system of quiz and progress testing.
proceed in our teaching as though only the minority
ents should be able to learn what we have to teach.
nothing sacred about the normal curve. It is the dis-
st appropriate to chance and random activity. Educa-
urposeful activity and we seek to have the students
we have to teach. If we are effective in our instruction
tion of achievement should be very different from the
ve. In fact, we may even insist that our educational
been *unsuccessful* to the extent to which our dis-
achievement approximates the normal distribution.
ial differences" in learners is a fact that can be demon-
many ways. That students vary in many ways can
orgotten. That these varations must be reflected in
ndards and achievement criteria is a reflection of our
practices rather than the necessities of the case. The
in education is to find strategies which will take in-
fferences into consideration but which will do so in
as to promote the fullest development of the individual.

II. THE VARIABLES FOR MASTERY
LEARNING STRATEGIES

strategy for mastery may be derived from the work of
63), supported by the ideas of Morrison (1926),
66), Skinner (1954), Suppes (1966), Goodlad and
1959), and Glaser (1968). In presenting these ideas
r to some of the research findings which bear on them.
ur main concern here is with the major variables in
school learning and the ways in which these variables
ized in a strategy for mastery learning.
briefest form, the model proposed by Carroll (1963)

ONE

BENJAMIN S. BLOOM

MASTERY LEARNING AND
ITS IMPLICATIONS FOR
CURRICULUM DEVELOPMENT

I. INTRODUCTION

Each teacher begins a new term — or course — with the expectation that about a third of his students will adequately learn what
he has to teach. He expects about a third of his students to fail
or to just "get by." Finally, he expects another third to learn a
good deal of what he has to teach, but not enough to be regarded
as "good students." This set of expectations, supported by school
policies and practices in grading, becomes transmitted to the students through the grading procedures and through the methods
and materials of instruction. This system creates a self-fulfilling
prophecy such that the final sorting of students through the grading process becomes approximately equivalent to the original
expectations.

This set of expectations, which fixes the academic goals of
teachers and students, is the most wasteful and destructive aspect
of the present educational system. It reduces the aspirations of
both teachers and students, it reduces motivation for learning in
students, and it systematically destroys the ego and self-concept
of a sizeable group of the students who are legally required to
attend school for ten to twelve years under conditions which are
frustrating and humiliating year after year. The cost of this system in reducing opportunities for further learning and in alienating

youth from both school and society is so great that no society can tolerate it for long.

Most students (perhaps over 90 per cent) can master what we have to teach them and it is the task of instruction to find the means which will enable our students to master the subject under consideration. A basic task is to determine what we mean by mastery of the subject and to search for the methods and materials which will enable the largest proportion of our students to attain such mastery.

Background. Some societies can utilize only a small number of highly educated persons in the economy and can provide the economic support for only a small proportion of the students to complete secondary or higher education. Under such conditions much of the effort of the schools and the external examining system is to find ways of rejecting the majority of students at various points in the educational system and to discover the talented few who are to be given advanced educational opportunities. Such societies invest a great deal more in the prediction and selection of talent than in the development of such talent.

The complexities of the skills required by the work force in the United States and in other highly developed nations means that we can no longer operate on the assumption that completion of secondary and advanced education is for the few. The increasing evidence (Schultz, 1963; Bowman, 1966) that investment in the education of humans pays off at a greater rate than does capital investment suggests that we cannot return to an economy of scarcity of educational opportunity.

Whatever might have been the case previously, highly developed nations must seek to find ways to increase the proportion of the age group that can successfully complete both secondary and higher education. The problem is no longer one of finding the few who can succeed. The basic problem is determining how the largest proportion of the age group can learn effectively those skills and subject matter regarded as essential for their own development in a complex society.

However, given another set of philosophic and psychological presuppositions, we may express our concern for the intellectual and personality consequences of lack of clear success in the learn-

ing tasks of the school. Increasingly [...]
tinuing learning) will be necessar[...]
the work force. If school learning [...]
even impossible by a sizeable pr[...]
can be done at later levels to kin[...]
learning. School learning must be [...]
basis for ensuring that learning [...]
life as needed.

Even more important in mode[...]
values. As the secular society be[...]
the values remaining for the indiv[...]
interpersonal relations, self-develo[...]
frustrate the students in the latt[...]
are available to the individual. [...]
each of these values, the schools [...]
of successful learning experience[...]
development.

There is little question that the [...]
ful learning experiences for som[...]
one-third of the students. If the [...]
and satisfying learning experienc[...]
students, major changes must t[...]
dents, teachers, and administrat[...]
in teaching strategies and in the [...]

The Normal Curv[...]
long used the normal curve in g[...]
to believe in it. Achievement [...]
differences among our learners — [...]
in terms of the subject matter. [...]
a normal fashion. In any grou[...]
some small per cent receive A [...]
percentage differs greatly from [...]
prepared to fail an equal prop[...]
this failure is determined by [...]
the group rather than by their [...]
of the course. Thus, we have [...]
students into about five categ[...]
to assigning grades in some r[...]

the fa[...]
C stud[...]
of one [...]

Hav[...]
set gr[...]
teache[...]
grades[...]
studen[...]
system [...]
Finally [...]
of our [...]

Ther[...]
tributio[...]
tion is [...]
learn w[...]
the dist[...]
normal [...]
efforts [...]
tributio[...]

"Indi[...]
strated [...]
never b[...]
learning [...]
policies [...]
basic ta[...]
dividual [...]
such a w[...]

A learnir[...]
Carroll ([...]
Bruner ([...]
Anderson[...]
we will re[...]
However, [...]
a model [...]
may be u[...]
Put in [...]

makes it clear that if the students are normally distributed with respect to *aptitude* for some subject (mathematics, science, literature, history, etc.) and all the students are provided with exactly the *same instruction* (same in terms of amount of instruction, quality of instruction, and time available for learning) the end result will be a normal distribution on an appropriate measure of achievement. Furthermore, the relation between aptitude and achievement will be relatively high (correlations of +.70 or higher are to be expected if the aptitude and achievement measures are valid and reliable). Conversely, if the students are normally distributed with respect to aptitude, but the kind and quality of instruction and the amount of time available for learning are made appropriate to the characteristics and needs of *each* student, the majority of students may be expected to achieve mastery of the subject. And, the relation between aptitude and achievement should approach zero. It is this basic set of ideas we wish to develop in the following material.

A. Aptitude for Particular Kinds of Learning. Teachers have come to recognize that individuals do differ in their aptitudes for particular kinds of learning and over the years test makers have developed a large number of aptitude tests to measure these differences. In study after study it has been found that aptitude tests are relatively good predictors of achievement criteria (achievement tests or teacher judgments). Thus, a good set of mathematics aptitude tests given at the beginning of the year will correlate as high as +.70 with the mathematics achievement tests given at the end of the course in algebra, or some other mathematics subject.

The use of aptitude tests for predictive purposes and the high correlations between such tests and achievement criteria have led many of us to the view that high levels of achievement are possible only for the most able students. From this, it is an easy step to some notion of a causal connection between aptitude and achievement. The simplest notion of causality is that the students with high levels of aptitude can learn the complex ideas of the subject while the students with low levels of aptitude can learn only the simplest ideas of the subject.

Quite in contrast to this is Carroll's (1963) view that *aptitude is the amount of time required by the learner to attain mastery of a learning task.* Implicit in this formulation is the assumption that, given enough time, all students can conceivably attain mastery of a learning task. If Carroll is right, then learning mastery is theoretically available to all, if we can find the means for helping each student. This formulation of Carroll's has the most fundamental implications for education.

One type of support for this view is to be found in the grade norms for many standardized achievement tests. These norms demonstrate that selected criterion scores achieved by the top students at one grade level are achieved by the majority of students at a later grade level. Further support is available in studies where students can learn at their own rate. These studies show that although most students eventually reach mastery on each learning task, some students achieve mastery much sooner than other students (Glaser, 1968; Atkinson, 1967).

Can all students learn a subject equally well? That is, can all students master a learning task at a high level of complexity? From a study of aptitude distributions in relation to student performance, we have become convinced that there are differences between the extreme students and the remainder of the population. At the top of the aptitude distribution (1 to 5 per cent) are likely to be some students who have a special talent for the subject. Such students are able to learn and to use the subject with greater fluency than other students. The student with special aptitudes for music or foreign languages can learn these subjects in ways not available to most other students. Whether this is a matter of native endowment or the effect of previous training is not clear, although this must vary from subject to subject. It is likely that some individuals are born with sensory organs better attuned to sounds (music, language, etc.) than are others and that these constitutional characteristics give them special advantages in learning such subjects over others. For other subjects, special training, particular interests, etc., may develop these high-level aptitudes.

At the other extreme of the aptitude distribution, there are individuals with special disabilities for particular learning. The tone-deaf individual will have great difficulty in learning music; the color-blind individual will have special problems in learning art; the individual who thinks in concrete forms will have special problems in learning highly abstract conceptual systems such as philosophy. Again, it is believed these may constitute less than

5 per cent of the distribution, but this will vary with the subject and the aptitudes.

In between are approximately 90 per cent of the individuals where the writer believes, as does Carroll, that aptitudes are predictive of the rate of learning rather than the level (or complexity) of learning that is possible. Thus, we are expressing the view that, given sufficient time (and appropriate types of help), 95 per cent of students — the top 5 per cent plus the next 90 per cent — can learn a subject up to a high level of mastery. We are convinced that the grade of A as an index of mastery of a subject can, under appropriate conditions, be achieved by up to 95 per cent of the students in a class.

It is assumed that it will take some students more effort, time, and help to achieve this level than it will other students. For some students the effort and help required may make it prohibitive. Thus, to learn high school algebra to a point of mastery may require a year or more for some students but only a fraction of a year for other students. Whether mastery learning is worth this great effort for the students who may need the longer time is highly questionable. One basic problem for a mastery learning strategy is to find ways of reducing the amount of time required by the slower students to a point where it is no longer a prohibitively long and difficult task for these less able students.

It is not assumed that aptitude for particular learning tasks is completely stable. There is evidence (Bloom, 1964; Hunt, 1961) that the aptitude for particular learning tasks may be modified by appropriate environmental conditions or learning experiences in the school and the home. The major task of educational programs concerned with learning to learn and general education should be to produce positive changes in the students' basic aptitudes. It is likely that these aptitudes can be most markedly affected during the early years in the home and during the elementary years of school. Undoubtedly, however, some changes can take place at later points in the individual's career.

However, even if marked changes are not made in the individual's aptitudes it is highly probable that more effective learning conditions can reduce the amount of time required to learn a subject to mastery for all students and especially for the students with lower aptitudes. It is this problem which must be directly attacked by strategies for mastery learning.

B. Quality of Instruction. The schools have usually proceeded on the assumption that there is a standard classroom situation for all students. Typically, this has been expressed in the teacher-student ratio of one to thirty, with group instruction as the central means of teaching. There is the expectation that each teacher will teach the subject in much the same way as other teachers. This standardization is further emphasized by textbook adoption which specifies the instructional material to be provided each class. Closely related to this is the extensive research over the past fifty years which seeks to find the one instructional method, material, or curriculum program that is best for all students.

Thus, over the years, researchers have fallen into the "educational trap" of specifying quality of instruction in terms of good and poor teachers, teaching, instructional materials, curriculum — all in terms of group results. They persist in asking such questions as: Who is the best teacher for the group? What is the best method of instruction for the group? What is the best instructional material for the group?

One may start with the very different assumption that individual students may need very different types and qualities of instruction to achieve mastery. That is, the same content and objectives of instruction may be learned by different students as the result of very different types of instruction. Carroll (1963) defines the *quality of instruction in terms of the degree to which the presentation, explanation, and ordering of elements of the task to be learned approach the optimum for a given learner.*

Much research is needed to determine how individual differences in learners can be related to variations in the quality of instruction. There is evidence that some students can learn quite well through independent learning efforts while others need highly structured teaching-learning situations (Congreve, 1965). It seems reasonable to expect that some students will need more concrete illustrations and explanations than will others; some students may need more examples to get an idea than do others; some students may need more approval and reinforcement than others; and some students may need to have several repetitions of the explanation while others may be able to get it the first time.

We believe that if every student had a very good tutor, most of them would be able to learn a particular subject to a high degree. It is the good tutor who attempts to find the qualities of instruction (and motivation) best suited to a given learner. And, there is some evidence (Dave, 1963) that middle-class parents do attempt to tutor their children when they believe that the quality of instruction in school is inadequate in a particular subject. In an unpublished study, the writer found that one-third of the students in an algebra course in a middle-class school were receiving as much tutorial instruction in the home in algebra as they were receiving group instruction in the school. These students received relatively high grades for the algebra course. For these students, the relationship between their mathematics aptitude scores at the beginning of the year and their achievement in algebra at the end of the year was almost zero. In contrast, for the students who received no additional instruction other than the regular classroom instruction, the relationship between their mathematics aptitude scores and their algebra achievement scores was very high ($+.90$). While this type of research needs to be replicated, it is evident in this small study that the home tutoring help was providing the quality of instruction needed by these students to learn the algebra — that is, the instruction was adapted to the needs of the individual learners.

The main point to be stressed is that the quality of instruction is to be considered in terms of its effects on individual learners rather than on random groups of learners. One hopes that the research of the future may lead to the definition of the qualities and kinds of instruction needed by various *types* of learners. Such research may suggest more effective group instruction since it is unlikely that the schools will be able to provide instruction for each learner separately.

C. Ability to Understand Instruction. In most courses at the high school and college level there is a single teacher and a single set of instructional materials. If the student has facility in understanding the teacher's communications about the learning and the instructional material (usually a textbook), he has little difficulty in learning the subject. If he has difficulty in understanding the teacher's instruction and/or the instructional material, he is likely to have great difficulty in learning the subject. *The ability to understand instruction may be defined as the ability of the learner to understand the nature of the task he is to learn and the procedures he is to follow in the learning of the task.*

Here is a point at which the students' abilities interact with the instructional materials and the instructor's abilities in teaching. For the student in our highly verbal schools it is likely that this ability to understand instruction is primarily determined by verbal ability and reading comprehension. These two measures of language ability are significantly related to achievement in the majority of subjects and they are highly related (+.50 to +.60) to grade-point averages at the high school or college level. What this suggests is that verbal ability (independent of specific aptitudes for each subject) determines some general ability to learn from teachers and instructional materials.

While it is possible to alter an individual's verbal ability by appropriate training, there are limits to the amount of change that can be produced. Most change in verbal ability can be produced at the pre-school and elementary school levels, with less and less change being likely as the student gets older (Bloom, 1964). However, vocabulary and reading ability may be improved to some extent at all age levels, even though there is diminishing utility to this approach with increasing age. Improvements in verbal abilities should result in improvements in the individual's ability to understand instruction.

The greatest immediate payoff in dealing with the ability to understand instruction is likely to come from modifications in instruction in order to meet the needs of individual students. There is no doubt that some teachers do attempt to modify their instruction to fit a given group of students. Many teachers center their instruction at the middle group of their students, others at the top or bottom group. These choices are, however, only reflections of the teacher's habits and attitudes; they are by no means determinants of what it is *possible* for a teacher to do. Given help and various types of aids, individual teachers can find ways of modifying their instruction to fit the differing needs of their students.

Group-study procedures should be available to students as they need it. In our own experience we have found that small groups of students (two or three students) meeting regularly to go over points of difficulty in the learning process were most effective, especially when the students could cooperate and help each other without any danger of giving each other special advantages in a competitive situation. Where learning can be turned into a co-operative process with everyone likely to gain from the process, small-group learning procedures can be very effective.

Tutorial help (one to one relations between teacher and learner) represents the most costly type of help and should be used only where alternative procedures are not effective. However, this type of help should be available to students as they need it, especially where individuals have particular difficulties that can't be corrected in other ways. The tutor, ideally, should be someone other than the teacher, since he should bring a fresh way of viewing the idea or the process. The tutor must be skillful in detecting the points of difficulty in the student's learning and should help him in such a way as to free the student from continued dependence on him.

Throughout the use of alternative methods of instruction and instructional material, the essential point to be borne in mind is that these are attempts to improve the *quality of instruction* in relation to the ability of each student to *understand the instruction*. As feedback methods inform the teachers of particular errors and difficulties the majority of students are having, it is to be expected that the regular group instruction could be modified so as to correct these difficulties. As particular students are helped individually, the goal should be not only to help the student over particular learning difficulties but also to enable him to become more independent in his learning and to help him identify the alternative ways by which he can comprehend new ideas.

D. Perseverance.

Carroll defines perseverance as *the time the learner is willing to spend in learning*. Obviously, if a student needs to spend a certain amount of time to master a particular task, and he spends less than this amount in active learning, he is not likely to learn the task to the level of mastery. Carroll attempts to differentiate between spending time on learning and the amount of time the student is actively engaged in learning.

There is no doubt that students vary in the amount of perseverance they bring to a specific learning task. However, students appear to approach different learning tasks with different amounts of perseverance. The student who gives up quickly in his efforts to learn an academic subject may persevere an unusually long time in learning how to repair an automobile or in learning to play a musical instrument. It would appear to us that as a student finds the effort rewarding, he is likely to spend more time on a particular learning task. If, on the other hand, the student is frustrated in his learning, he must — in self-defense — reduce the amount of time he devotes to the learning. While the frustration level of students may vary, we believe that all students must sooner or later give up a task if it is too painful for them.

While efforts may be made to increase the amount of perseverance in students, it is likely that manipulation of the instruction and learning materials may be more effective in helping students master a given learning task, in spite of their present level of perseverance. Frequency of reward and evidence of success in learning can increase the student's perseverance in a learning situation. As students attain mastery of a given task, they are likely to increase their perseverance for a related learning task.

Research at Chicago is showing that the demands for perseverance may be sharply reduced if students are provided with the instructional resources most appropriate for them. Frequent feedback accompanied by specific help in instruction and material as needed can reduce the time (and perseverance) required. Improvement in the quality of instruction or of the explanations and illustrations may reduce the amount of perseverance necessary for a given learning task.

There seems to be little reason to make learning so difficult that only a small proportion of the students can persevere to mastery. Endurance and unusual perseverance may be appropriate for long distance running; they are not great virtues in their own right. The emphasis should be on learning, not on vague ideas of discipline and endurance.

         E.   Time Allowed for Learning. Throughout the world schools are organized to give group instruction, with definite periods of time allocated for particular learning tasks. A course in history at the secondary level may be planned for an academic year of instruction, another course may be planned for a semester, while the amount of instructional time allocated for a subject like arithmetic at the fifth grade may be fixed. Whatever the amount of time allowed by the school and the curriculum for particular subjects or learning tasks, it is likely to be too much for some students and not enough for others.

For Carroll, the time spent on learning is the key to mastery. His basic assumption is that aptitude determines the rate of learning and that most, if not all students can achieve mastery if they devote the amount of time needed to the learning. This implies not only that the student must spend the amount of time he needs on the learning task but also that he be *allowed* enough time for the learning to take place.

There seems to be little doubt that students with high levels of aptitude are likely to be more efficient in their learning and to require less time for learning than students with lower levels of aptitude. Whether most students can be helped to become highly efficient learners in general is a problem for future research.

The amount of time students need for a particular kind of learning has not been studied directly. One indication of the time needed comes from studies of the amount of time students spend on homework. In reviewing the amount of time spent by 13-year-old students on mathematics homework in the International Study of Educational Achievement (Husén, 1967), we find that if we omit the extreme 5 per cent of the subjects, the ratio is roughly six to one. That is, some students spend six times as much time on mathematics homework as do others. Other studies of student use of time suggest that this is roughly the order of magnitude to be expected.

If instruction and student use of time become more effective, it is likely that most students will need less time to learn the subject to mastery and the ratio of time required for the slower and the faster learners may be reduced from about six to one to perhaps three to one.

We are convinced that it is not the sheer amount of time spent in learning — either in school or out of school — that accounts for the level of learning. Each student should be allowed the time he needs to learn a subject. And, the time he needs to learn the subject is likely to be affected by the student's aptitudes, his verbal ability, the quality of instruction he receives in class, and the quality of the help he receives out of class. The task of a strategy for mastery learning is to find ways of altering the time individual students need for learning as well as to find ways of providing

whatever time is needed by each student. Thus, a strategy for
mastery learning must find some way of solving the instructional
problems as well as the school organizational problems, including
that of time.

III. WHY MASTERY LEARNING?

The curriculum maker in the past did not have to contend with
the many problems raised by mastery learning. He attempted to
devise what he believed to be an effective curriculum for the
teaching of selected subjects and he was quite prepared to accept
a high rate of failure or at least a sizeable proportion of students
who just got by with some low minimum of learning. However,
when one faces the possibility that "all" should be able to learn,
curriculum making is confronted with the problem of why all
should learn any specific subject. What is so important that all
should learn?

Parents (and even curriculum makers) have no difficulty in
accepting mastery learning as important when physical survival
is at stake. A parent teaching his child to cross the road safely,
or to avoid dangerous situations such as fire, poison, use of dangerous tools, machinery, and equipment, etc., is not content with
partial learning. He will spend the necessary time, use the reinforcement he believes appropriate, and evaluate the child's behavior in the situation until he is fully assured that the child has
mastered the learning. One could cite many examples of mastery
learning in the home, industry, and even in military training where
the instructor insists that all learners reach an acceptable level
of mastery before instruction ceases. These examples are usually
seen as so important for the physical survival of the individual
learner that the teacher (or parent) takes it for granted that less
than mastery of the learning task is unacceptable.

More recently we have begun to realize the relation between
economic survival (at least a decent standard of life) and the
development of certain abilities, skills, interests, and aptitudes.
Some of these may be learned on the job while others may be prerequisites to employment in satisfactory occupations. As we come
to recognize the minimal language skills, cognitive abilities, and
affective characteristics necessary for economic survival, the curriculum maker must become preoccupied with the means by which

mastery of these behaviors can be developed in all or almost all students.

In a complex society such as ours there are a variety of citizenship skills, understandings, interests, and attitudes that may be necessary for the individual to lead a satisfying life and for the nation to survive as a democratic and open society. Such kinds of behavior become more difficult to define and to set standards for, but they too require at least minimal levels of mastery.

While I have by no means exhausted the consideration of the types of behavior or subjects for which mastery learning may provide survival benefits in a complex society, there is another type of criteria for justification of mastery in learning. In addition to the overt and substantive curriculum with which the curriculum makers and teachers are preoccupied, there is a latent or covert curriculum which may be equally important from the viewpoint of the learner. The learner comes to view himself as adequate or inadequate in terms of his effectiveness in learning what the school or curriculum expects of him. Whether the learning task be important or trivial, the learner judges his own adequacy as a human in terms of his effectiveness relative to other learners. He is judged by teachers, examinations, and his own peers on the basis of his success — or lack of it — in the learning tasks set by the school and the curriculum. These judgments which are communicated to him in the classroom and the school are further reinforced by his parents. For the student to consistently get low grades or perform poorly in school is to become frustrated and to develop a negative self-concept. On the other hand, to consistently do well in school over a number of years is likely to lead to the development of a feeling of adequacy and a positive self-image. Mastery learning, then, helps to provide the individual with the basis for positive ego development and a sense of adequacy. Thus, one may justify mastery learning in terms of its opening up of interests in further learning and its developing of a positive attitude toward school and school learning, as well as of a healthy self-concept. There is evidence that mental health is promoted by success in school learning, whereas repeated failure or lack of success in school learning is a source of anxiety and, over a period of time, a source of infection with respect to mental illness.

All of this is to suggest that mastery learning notions are relatively easy to comprehend and accept where the survival and well-being of the individual in the society are at issue. It is where the schools and the curriculum makers are not really convinced of the importance of what they have to teach that they have difficulty in deciding on standards to be reached and that they become satisfied if a few of the learners really do learn what is being taught.

In the past, a small proportion of "successful" learners were identified for further learning. In a society where all the learners are expected to complete ten to twelve years of learning, where as high as 50 to 60 per cent of the learners are expected to secure some form of higher education, and where almost all individuals are expected to continue learning throughout life, obviously we can no longer be satisfied when only some small proportion of learners adequately learn what the schools have to teach. Increasingly, curriculum makers and teachers are going to be judged in terms of the proportion of the learners who have "mastered" the learning tasks of the school as well as the proportion of students who develop a positive self-concept through their interaction with the school environment.

IV. WHERE IS MASTERY LEARNING MOST APPROPRIATE?

In our experience so far, mastery learning has been relatively easy to achieve in school subjects with a minimum of prerequisites. For example, first-year algebra has a minimum of specific prerequisites and therefore a one-year course with appropriate feedback and corrective techniques has been especially successful in bringing the large majority of students up to a given standard of mastery. Similarly, secondary school courses in biology and chemistry have been relatively successful from the viewpoint of mastery learning. College courses in statistics, introductory psychology, biology, and even philosophy have also been effective from this viewpoint.

Although we do not have information about mastery strategies in many subject areas, we doubt the likelihood that a seventh- or eighth-grade arithmetic course could reach acceptable levels of mastery learning with a heterogeneous group of learners, because such courses depend heavily on the mastery of earlier concepts and skills in the arithmetic program from grades one to six. Likewise, we believe it easier to secure mastery learning in a first course in a second language than in a course in the mother tongue because of the greater heterogeneity of the students in the prerequisite skills and abilities at the beginning of the course in the mother tongue.

Thus, we are arguing that relatively quick demonstrations of effective mastery learning may be achieved in courses where a large portion of the learners have the minimal prerequisite learning at the time of entrance to the course or where the subject demands relatively little in the way of specific prerequisite learning.

We are convinced that it would be possible to organize an entire curriculum over many years (e.g., grades one to six, nine to twelve, etc.) where students could achieve mastery learning each year as they progressed through the curriculum. And, we suggest that developmental and research efforts be instituted to bring about such results, because mastery learning at these critical ages and grades could make for more effective learning throughout the student's educational career. And, even more important is the likelihood that early mastery learning could have long-term consequences on the individual's self-concept and mental health.

In spite of these considerations of where mastery learning is easier or more difficult to produce, there are more fundamental considerations of where mastery learning is appropriate or inappropriate. Clearly, not all school subjects need strive for mastery learning, and perhaps not all students should strive for mastery learning in all subjects.

It would seem to us that subjects which are *required, sequential, closed,* and which emphasize *convergent thinking* should, insofar as possible, employ mastery learning strategies. Perhaps we can explain these points briefly.

If a subject is *required* of the learners, then someone has regarded it as important for the learners or for the society, and better or more adequate learning of such a subject is to be preferred to a lesser level of learning. If a subject is required we believe that the learner should be given every opportunity to succeed in it and, conversely, the learner's failure in a required subject should be seen as a defect in the curriculum and/or the instruction. We believe that a high rate of failure (or a low level of learning) in a required subject needlessly inflicts a negative self-concept on a group of learners who have no choice about being in the learning situation or course. Since about two-thirds of the K through 12 curriculum in the United States is required, we are expressing the view that at least this portion of the curriculum should employ mastery learning strategies.

An even better case can be made for mastery learning in *sequential* subjects. If learning of some set of school subjects (arithmetic, language arts, mathematics, etc.) is sequential in the sense that the second course builds on — and requires — the first course (and the third course builds on the first two courses, etc.), then the student should be assured of successful progress through the sequence, insofar as this is possible. This, of course, places a very heavy burden on the first course, since inadequate learning in this course almost assures inadequate learning in each of the subsequent courses in the sequence. Mastery learning thus requires a greater concern on the part of the curriculum maker about sequence and more careful consideration of what is truly sequential in learning and why. In the first criterion (that of required courses), we believe that it is in some ways *immoral* to permit inadequacies in the curriculum or instruction "to fail" students where they have no choice about what learning tasks they are to do. For our second criterion, we believe that it is *inefficient* to permit inadequacies in the curriculum or instruction to produce low levels of learning in a sequential arrangement of learning tasks where adequate levels of learning in the earlier part of a sequence make it highly probable that the students will be able to learn the later parts of the sequence to relatively high levels of adequacy.

By *closed* subjects we mean subjects where there is a finite set of ideas and behaviors to be learned about which there is considerable agreement among curriculum makers and teachers. A closed subject is also one which is unlikely to change much over a decade or more. For example, arithmetic and mathematics may be regarded as relatively closed subjects. Even though there may be much change in the methods of teaching these subjects, their content and behaviors do not change fundamentally. History, many science courses, second-language courses, and, to a lesser extent, mother tongue courses may also be regarded as closed subjects. Here the arguments for mastery learning stem from the relative ease with which mastery learning standards can be developed, the general consensus about what learning is important for the students to acquire, and the great likelihood that once mastery learning strategies have been adequately developed for one generation or group of learners they can be employed for subsequent cycles of learners and teachers.

Finally, we believe that courses which emphasize *convergent thinking,* that is, thinking for which there are "right answers," "good solutions," and "appropriate thought processes" should employ mastery learning strategies. The argument here again stems from the ease with which mastery learning standards can be derived and the availability of considerable consensus not only about the *products* of thinking (and learning) but also about the *processes* of thinking that should be developed. Here again, subjects like mathematics, history, much of language arts, and second-language courses are believed to be appropriate for mastery learning since convergent thinking appears to be the major behavior which is emphasized in such courses.

Space and time considerations suggest that I leave it to the reader to determine whether or not arguments for mastery learning are less compelling for elective courses, for non-sequential learning tasks, for "open" subjects, and for courses that emphasize divergent thinking and creativity. While I believe that mastery learning strategies could — and should — be employed in such courses, I do admit that it is more difficult to determine standards and criteria and I suspect it is more difficult to develop appropriate mastery learning strategies for such courses and for the students in them.

Perhaps another way of looking at the same problem is to point out that highly centralized curriculum development efforts are usually invested in subjects which are required, sequential, closed, and which emphasize convergent thinking. While teachers clearly do have considerable influence on the effectiveness of learning in such subjects, it is the curriculum maker who must bear the burden of demonstrating what can and should be learned by the students. And, it is the curriculum maker who must find the strategies which will insure that the largest proportion of students will learn adequately if the curriculum and its materials and methods are used properly. It is the curriculum maker who must develop in-service training programs to insure that teacher inadequacy or misunderstanding is not responsible for the failure of the curriculum or the students. And, we assert here that it is the curriculum maker who must develop the variety of alternative learning materials required for mastery learning as well as the measurement materials needed to support a given strategy for mastery learning.

V. MEASUREMENT SYSTEM

Curriculum makers during the past fifteen years have come to recognize that existing standardized tests are not valid for a basically new curriculum. As a result, they were instrumental in designing and/or constructing new evaluation procedures which had high content validity for the new curriculum. Thus, the traditional separation of curriculum and evaluation has been reduced or eliminated.

If mastery learning is to be effective for the schools, the curriculum maker must become involved in creating a measurement system which will serve the needs of teachers and students. Such a measurement system should include the following: (a) placement and pre-tests; (b) measures of aptitudes, cognitive styles, and reinforcement patterns; (c) summative evaluation; (d) formative evaluation; and (e) affective evaluation procedures.

A. Placement and Pre-Tests. Teachers persist in viewing students as though they begin a course with similar background and achievement characteristics. They believe they are offering all an "equal" opportunity to learn the subject. For most school subjects, appropriate placement and pre-tests reveal great variation in the relevant previous learning. These variations have significant consequences for the success or failure of the student in learning the next subject.

Probably the most important use of placement or pre-tests is to reveal the extent to which the students have mastered the important prerequisites for a particular approach to a subject. If a course in chemistry, for example, assumes a specific level of competency in mathematics, then it is likely that students who do not possess the appropriate mathematical competency will do poorly in the chemistry, not because they can't learn chemistry but because they can't learn chemistry taught in a particular way. The placement tests should give indications of what may be needed, such as teaching the prerequisite skills before the students enter the course, offering several versions of the subject built on different sets of prerequisites, or instructing the students on the prerequisite skills as part of the course.

The use of placement tests is especially important in a sequence of learning extending over several years, such as arithmetic, language, mathematics, science, etc. Here it is necessary to determine just where each student is in the sequence so that he may be placed in those learning tasks which are appropriate for him. If he is placed too far ahead of his position in the sequence or too far behind, he is not likely to learn well or to learn productively. Placement tests have been used in the past primarily for placing transfer students and for grouping students. Here we are concerned with the use of placement tests as a basis for determining the appropriate next learning experiences for each student, whether the instruction is individualized or grouped.

Much work is needed to determine just how placement tests should be constructed and used so as to offer the appropriate diagnosis and educational prescription for each student. This question presents serious theoretical and practical problems in evaluations, and for teachers and curriculum developers. The effective use of mastery learning strategies is dependent on the availability and use of well-developed placement and pre-tests.

B. Measures of Aptitudes, Cognitive Styles, and Reinforcement Patterns. There is a great deal of evidence that students vary in the ways in which they study and learn. However, we have rarely taken advantage of these differences in designing instructional materials or in selecting and using instructional procedures. Most of our instructional material and instructional methods are designed to give great advantage to students who are high in verbal ability. Some of us believe it is possible to design instruction so as to give advantage to students who are high in other aptitudes.

Perhaps the implications of this can be made clearer. If we use the usual intelligence test with a single summary score, and define the upper 10 per cent as gifted, then by definition only 10 per cent of the student population can be regarded as gifted. If, on the other hand, we use a battery of aptitude tests, such as the seven primary mental abilities, then as high as 50 per cent of the student population will be found to be gifted (in the upper 10 per cent) on one or more of these aptitude tests. Undoubtedly, the proportion of gifted students by such a definition would be as high as 95 per cent if we included enough aptitudes.

Our problem is not that there isn't enough giftedness in the student population, it is that we don't know how to use most of these aptitudes as a basis for designing instructional methods and materials.

Some of our students are beginning to provide some clues for solutions to these instructional problems. For example, in one study we found that the rate of learning a set of logical reasoning tasks was largely determined by the spatial orientation abilities of the students. We were somewhat puzzled by this discovery, since in the past, spatial orientation was rarely of value in predicting achievement or rate of learning of school subjects. However, the author of this study was able to defend his data by explaining the way in which he had taught logical reasoning. He had used Venn diagrams as the basis for teaching syllogistic reasoning — a method of instruction which made excellent use of spatial orientation abilities. We are trying to persuade some of our students to extend this research to demonstrate methods of teaching logical reasoning which will give special advantage to students high in numerical aptitude or memory or verbal ability, or even reasoning ability. We believe it should be possible to design instructional procedures and materials which can give advantage to selected abilities and put other abilities at a disadvantage. Clearly, this will require great ingenuity on the part of the designer of instruction and instructional material.

We do not believe that the usual psychological aptitudes will provide the best basis for designing instructional strategies. It is most likely that cognitive styles, or some more direct approach to observing the ways in which students study and learn will help us discover the particular learning aptitudes which are more basic for determining the types of instruction needed.

A final word as to reinforcement patterns. Some of the work being done at the University of Hawaii suggests that what the teacher believes to be the rewards which influence students positively may under some conditions have the opposite effect. This research indicates that there may be almost as much variation in the reinforcers that influence students as there is in the aptitudes they possess. Eventually, we must find techniques for appraising the reinforcers for individuals. And, of course, we must find methods of helping teachers learn to use a greater variety of reinforcers as well as to relate reinforcers to individual needs.

   C. Summative Evaluation. In order to develop mastery learning in students, one must be able to recognize when students have achieved it. Teachers must be able to define what they mean by mastery and they must be able to collect the necessary evidence to establish whether or not a student has achieved it.

The specification of the objectives and content of instruction is one necessary precondition for informing both teachers and students about the expectations. The translation of the specifications into evaluation procedures helps to define further what it is that the student should be able to do when he has completed the course. The evaluation procedures used to appraise the outcomes of instruction (summative evaluation) help the teacher and student know when the instruction has been effective.

Implicit in this way of defining the outcomes and preparing evaluation instruments is a distinction between the teaching-learning process and the evaluation process. At some point in time, the results of teaching and learning can be reflected in the evaluation of the students. But, these are *separate* processes. That is, teaching and learning are intended to prepare the student in an area of learning, while evaluation (summative) is intended to appraise the extent to which the student has developed in the desired ways. Both the teacher and the learner must have some understanding of what the achievement criteria are and both must be able to secure evidence of progress toward these criteria.

Mastery learning requires summative evaluation procedures that have high validity generally and that are clearly relevant (have content validity) to the specific instruction and course under consideration. If teachers are to change their grading procedures they must have great confidence in the evaluation procedures on which the grades are to be based.

It is probable that standardized tests of the kind we have known over the past 40 years are less likely to be relevant for this purpose — primarily because they are intended for widespread use and because they rarely fit well the local conditions. On the other hand, few teachers are confident enough of their own examining procedures to trust their own examinations for this purpose.

What the teachers need is a supply of test items and testing procedures in which they can have confidence but which fit local conditions of instruction and curriculum. Several groups in the United States and England are attempting to construct item pools or item banks which can be used by teachers to assemble their own evaluation instruments. These consist of from 500 to 1,000 test questions constructed very carefully to fit the major objectives of instruction for a particular subject or set of courses. Each item is carefully developed to meet the instructional specifications; it is tried out and revised on the basis of appropriate data; it is then placed in the item bank so as to be identifiable by content, behavior, and level of difficulty; and, where relevant it is also indexed by learning units in commonly used textbooks and courses of study. Item pools may be developed by combinations of teachers, evaluation experts, and curriculum specialists. These pools should be continually modified and expanded to include the important cognitive, affective, and psychomotor objectives in a subject. They must be put in such a form that teachers can use them easily and efficiently. And, they should be designed to make evaluation practices in the classroom approximate the highest state of the art in a particular subject, rather than to perpetuate the relatively mediocre evaluation practices revealed by various surveys of the test practices used by teachers in the classrooms at present. It is clear that much in-service education will be needed if teachers are to make good use of item banks.

One problem which is posed by mastery learning is that of determining standards of mastery. Our present standardized tests have excellent normative data based on carefully selected national, regional, or state samples. For mastery learning we will need criterion reference standards; that is, standards which will reflect a criterion of what is meant by mastery or adequate achievement. At present, there are no very clear methods of arriving at such standards other than by the use of expert judgments — and this still leaves open the problem of what constitutes an expert and how the experts are to make and combine their judgments. One approach to the creation of criterion-referenced norms is to apply the standards arrived at in one year (or in one group) to other groups of students. Thus, in some of our work, standards of grading used in 1965 were applied to parallel tests used in 1966 and 1967. In 1967, 90 per cent of the students were given a grade of A because they had done as well on the parallel tests as the 15 per cent of students who received a grade of A in 1965. Thus, the problem became one of creating parallel tests and of ensuring that particular standards used in one year were applied to the performance standards for other years. Much research will be needed before we have confidence in criterion reference standards. We believe that the mathematical models developed by George Rasch of Denmark may help guide us in this work.

> *D. Formative Evaluation.* Although summative evaluation is necessary to determine when students have attained mastery of a subject, it is not very useful in the process of developing mastery. Another type of evaluation is necessary to provide feedback to teachers and to students during the learning-teaching process. The term *formative evaluation,* first used by Scrivin (1967) in connection with curriculum development, has been used by us to refer to brief diagnostic-progress tests which can be used over relatively brief sets of learning tasks. In our work we have found it useful to think of learning units as involving a week or two of learning activity or as including a chapter in a textbook or a well-defined content portion of a course.

Using some of the ideas of Gagné (1965) and Bloom (1956), we analyzed each unit into a number of elements ranging from specific terms or facts, to more complex and abstract ideas such as concepts and principles, and then to relatively complex processes such as application of principles and analysis of complex theoretical statements. We assumed that these elements form a hierarchy of learning tasks.

We find that two independent experts reach over 90 per cent agreement in defining the elements included in an instructional unit as well as the hierarchical relations among the elements. When a set of test questions is constructed to evaluate achievement on the unit, the pattern of student responses on about three-fourths of the items fits the hypothesized hierarchy. Further research will be needed before our formative tests will have the level of construct validity we desire.

Each formative test is administered after the completion of the appropriate learning unit. While the frequency of these progress tests may vary throughout the course, it is likely that some portions of the course — and especially the early sections of the course — may need more frequent formative tests than later portions of the course. Where some of the learning units are basic and prerequisite for other units of the course, the tests should be frequent enough to insure thorough mastery of such learning material.

For those students who have thoroughly mastered the unit, the formative tests should reinforce the learning and assure the student that his present mode of learning and approach to study is adequate. Since he will have a number of such tests, the student who consistently demonstrates mastery should be able to reduce his anxiety about his course achievement.

For students who lack mastery of a particular unit, the formative tests should reveal the particular points of difficulty, that is, the specific questions they answered incorrectly and the particular ideas, skills, and processes they still need to work on. It is most helpful when the diagnosis shows the elements in a learning hierarchy that the students still need to learn. It has been observed that students respond best to the formative test results when they are referred to particular instructional materials or processes intended to help them correct their difficulties. The *diagnosis* should be accompanied by a very specific *prescription* if the students are to do anything about it.

These formative tests may also give feedback to teachers. In the work we have done in the schools, the teachers locate the items on which a large portion of the students (usually 65 per cent or more) have made errors. The ideas underlying these items are reviewed soon after the formative test has been given and the teachers attempt to explain the learning element in a different way, since the results on these items suggest that there must have been some difficulty in understanding the instructional material or the instructional process the first time during the class.

We believe that *formative evaluation* represents a basic new development in the nature and use of evaluation. Much must be done before the formative evaluation procedures will have the high level of validity and reliability that is common in carefully developed summative evaluation. More research is needed before we can determine the best procedures for using the formative tests by teachers and students and the conditions under which teachers and students will use the feedback provided by these instruments. What we have found so far is that formative tests can make the progress of students visible during the actual process of instruction and learning and that these evaluation instruments yield excellent estimates of what individual students (and groups of students) will do on the summative evaluation instruments given at the end of a term or year. The main point is that we can correct the learning (and the instruction) before it is too late.

    E.   Affective Evaluation Procedures. Education in this country as well as abroad has been primarily concerned with objectives in the cognitive domain. Affective characteristics such as interest in the subject, attitudes toward school learning, and attitudes toward the self have been evaluated only in major studies. Rarely do teachers concern themselves with such evaluation except when they observe student behavior so extreme that it cannot fail to be noticed.

Our studies and many studies in the literature find a relatively high relationship between a student's success in learning a subject and his interest in the subject. Whether the cognitive success is the cause of the interest in the subject or whether both develop concurrently is not entirely clear. However, we are quite clear that students who do well in a subject begin to "like" the subject and to desire more of it. To do well in a subject opens up further avenues for exploration of the subject. Conversely, to do poorly in a subject may close this area for further study. Interest in a subject is both a cause of mastery of the subject as well as a result of mastery. Motivation for further learning in a subject is one of the more important consequences of mastery.

So also is the attitude toward school and school learning. To do well generally in school is to like school generally and to have a positive attitude toward school learning. Conversely, to do poorly in school is so threatening to the individual in modern society that he must come to reject school at the first opportunity or to avoid further schooling if permitted.

At a deeper level is the question of a student's self-concept and his mental health. Each person searches for positive recognition of his worth and he comes to view himself as adequate in those areas where he receives assurance of his competence or success. Mastery and its public recognition (grades, honors, etc.) provide the necessary reassurance and reinforcement to help the student view himself as adequate.

In a longitudinal study over the elementary school period, one of our University of Chicago colleagues (Glidewell, 1967) found that there was a significant relationship between school marks and psychiatric measures of mental health. Similar relations were found between school marks and the individual's self concept. This writer concluded that although there had been a long fruitless search for immunization procedures in mental health analoguous to those found in physical health, the data supported the conclusion that success in school over a period of years does provide immunization against later mental illness. One may interpret these findings in a slightly different way. For the students who are roughly in the top third of their classes consistently, over a number of years, the school serves to build a positive self-concept and provides them with some immunization against later emotional stress. For these students, the school environment has a powerful positive effect not only in cognitive learning but also in the affective domain. However, for the students who are roughly in the bottom third of their classes, consistently over a number of years, the school serves to *infect* them with greatly lowered self-esteem and a lowered resistance to emotional stress. Thus, the school environment (especially when supported by the home environment) may have positive or negative effects not only in the cognitive development of the individual but also in his affective development.

Further work is being done in these areas to replicate previous research and also to determine the effects of mastery learning on these affective characteristics. What appears to be emerging is that the affective characteristics are influenced by the student's perception of his standing within the class or group and are relatively independent of his test standing on national norms. Thus, we encounter situations where two students in different classes have identical scores on a standardized achievement test, but one student is at the top of his class while the other student is at the bottom of his class. The affective characteristics of these students are very different — one positive and the other negative.

The point here is that the schools (and the curriculum developers) must assume responsibility for the affective as well as the cognitive development of students. We need evaluation instruments that will give us clear indications of the interests, attitudes, and mental health of the students, especially as these are influenced positively or negatively by classroom instruction, the larger school environment, and by our grading and other systems of rewarding or punishing students.

VI. A SYSTEM OF INSTRUCTIONAL SUPPORTS FOR BOTH TEACHERS AND LEARNERS

Variation in the student's ability to understand instruction must be met by providing alternative learning and instructional resources. Curriculum makers have already begun to attack this problem by developing a variety of instructional approaches to a particular learning task. We recognize that the curriculum makers and the schools must provide a system of instructional supports if mastery learning is to be attained by most students. Several types of support may be needed, including: (a) alternative learning resources; (b) student support for one another; and (c) teacher support for one another.

A.   Alternative Learning Resources. In our use of formative tests we have diagnosed the difficulties particular students had in a learning task and provided specific suggestions of materials the student could use to correct his difficulties. A variety of instructional materials helps both teachers and students overcome feelings of defeatism and passivity about learning. If the student cannot learn in one way, he should be reassured that alternatives are available to him. Teachers and curriculum specialists who participate in constructing formative tests have been very creative in suggesting (and developing) instructional materials which are helpful to students making particular errors on the formative tests. In the work in the schools, each student has access to a half-dozen or more alternative sets of learning materials. Some of the following types of instructional materials have been used.

Textbooks may vary in the clarity with which they explain a particular idea or process. The fact that one textbook has been adopted by the school or by the teacher does not necessarily mean that other textbooks cannot be used at particular points in the instruction when they would be helpful to a student who cannot grasp the idea from the adopted textbook. The task here is to be able to determine where the individual student has difficulty in understanding the instructions and then to provide alternative textbook explanations if they are more effective at that point.

Workbooks and programmed instruction units may be especially helpful for some students who can't grasp the ideas or a procedure in the textbook form. Some students need the drill and the specific tasks which workbooks can provide. Other students need the small steps and frequent reinforcement which programmed units can provide. Such materials may be used in the initial instruction or as students encounter specific difficulties in learning a particular unit or section of the course.

Audio-visual methods and academic games may help some students who learn a particular idea best through concrete illustrations and vivid and clear explanations. It is likely that film strips and short motion pictures which can be used by individual students as needed may be very effective. Other students may need concrete material such as laboratory experiences, simple demonstrations, blocks and other relevant apparatus in order to comprehend an idea or task. Academic games, puzzles, and other interesting but not threatening devices may be useful. Here again, the point is that some ways of communicating and comprehending an idea, problem, or task may be especially effective for some students although others may not use or need such materials and methods. We need not place the highest priority for all on abstract and verbal ways of instruction.

With regard to instructional materials, the suggestion is not that particular materials be used by particular students throughout the course. It is that each type of material may serve as a means of helping individual students at selected points in the learning process — and that a particular student may use whatever variety of materials are found to be useful as he encounters difficulties in the learning.

B. Student Support for One Another. The most effective procedure found thus far is to have small groups of students (3 or 4) meet regularly for as much as an hour per week to review the results of their formative tests and to help each other overcome the difficulties identified on their tests. In one set of schools, the entire class meets for one extra hour per week to do this. In other situations, the students meet on their own.

Clearly, the previous experiences of the students and their motivation determine the conditions under which they will best support and help each other.

        C. Teacher Support for One Another. We have found it useful to provide teachers with about four to six hours of orientation in the theory and procedures needed for mastery learning, followed by biweekly or monthly meetings to help each other as they encounter difficulties. Such meetings seem to be necessary to move to effective use of mastery learning procedures, to deal with the detailed problems of helping individual students, and to shift from one approach to another as the records on the formative tests are considered. Teachers are very effective in suggesting alternative approaches to particular problems and in helping one another maintain confidence in the students and in themselves.

VII. CREATION AND MAINTENANCE OF THE VIEW THAT ALL CAN LEARN

All of us have become convinced by years of experience that only a small group of students can really learn what we have to teach them. The view that all can learn is hard to accept since it calls into question what we have been doing in our teaching and grading. No series of lectures or administrative memoranda will change this. What is needed is a careful and clear demonstration that mastery learning is possible in key subjects of the curriculum. The type of research I have indicated can do this — and there is evidence that teachers who participate in research-demonstration efforts which are successful become enthusiastic and continue along these lines in subsequent teaching of the same courses. Students who learn well under mastery learning conditions also become enthusiastic and want these conditions in their other courses.

However, I believe that the creation of the view that all can learn to mastery levels requires time and ample demonstration before it is fully accepted as a guiding educational philosophy. If teachers participate in attacking these problems, aided by the types of support systems I have suggested, they will come to accept these ideas. Students (and their parents) will come to accept these ideas also when they are directly involved in successful mastery learning experiences.

But back of all this is the basic philosophy of the educational system itself. This goes back to our basic views about human nature and individual differences. Also, it goes back to our view of what is worth learning well. Where learning is for survival, we have no doubt that all can and must learn the subject to mastery. Our difficulty is that we are not certain that what we teach is that important. Should all learn algebra to mastery? What level of reading competence is necessary for all? When we are convinced of the importance of particular learning, we will have no difficulty in accepting mastery learning.

BIBLIOGRAPHY

R. C. Atkinson, "Computerized Instruction and the Learning Process," Technical Report No. 122, Stanford California: Institute for Mathematical Studies in the Social Sciences, 1967.

B. S. Bloom (ed.), *Taxonomy of Educational Objectives: Handbook I, Cognitive Domain,* New York: David McKay and Co., 1956.

B. S. Bloom, *Stability and Change in Human Characteristics,* New York: John Wiley and Sons, 1964.

M. J. Bowman, "The New Economics of Education," *International Journal of Educational Sciences,* Vol. 1, 1966, 29–46.

Jerome Bruner, *Toward a Theory of Instruction,* Cambridge: Harvard University Press, 1966.

John Carroll, "A Model of School Learning," *Teachers College Record,* Vol. 64, 1963, 723–33.

W. J. Congreve, "Independent Learning," *North Central Association Quarterly,* Vol. 40, 1965, 222–28.

R. H. Dave, "The identification and measurement of environmental process variables that are related to educational achievement," unpublished Ph.D. dissertation, University of Chicago, 1963.

Robert M. Gagné, *The Conditions of Learning,* New York: Holt, Rinehart, and Winston, 1965.

R. Glaser, "Adapting the Elementary School Curriculum to Individual Performance," *Proceedings* of the 1967 Invitational Conference on Testing Problems, Princeton, N.J.: Educational Testing Service, 1968.

J. I. Goodlad, and R. H. Anderson, *The Non-Graded Elementary School,* New York: Harcourt, Brace, and World, 1959.

J. McV. Hunt, *Intelligence and Experience,* New York: Ronald Press Co., 1961.

T. Husén (ed.), *International Study of Educational Achievement in Mathematics: A Comparison of Twelve Countries, Volumes I and II,* New York: John Wiley and Sons, 1967.

H. C. Morrison, *The Practice of Teaching in the Secondary School,* Chicago: University of Chicago Press, 1926.

T. W. Schultz, *The Economic Value of Education,* New York: Columbia University Press, 1963.

Michael Scriven, "The Methodology of Evaluation," in R. Stake (ed.), *Perspectives of Curriculum Evaluation,* Chicago: Rand McNally & Co, 1967.

B. F. Skinner, "The Science of Learning and the Art of Teaching," *Harvard Educational Review,* Vol. 24, 1954, 86–97.

P. Suppes, "The Uses of Computers in Education," *Scientific American,* Vol. 215, 1966, 206–21.

Lee J. Cronbach

Comments on

MASTERY LEARNING AND ITS IMPLICATIONS FOR CURRICULUM DEVELOPMENT

This is a splendid paper, eloquent and stimulating. I had better start my comments by noting that although Dr. Bloom and I have been arguing fine points of theology with each other since prehistoric times, we are both devout members of the same church. As I make critical points, you are going to think that my intention is to tear down the paper and refute what he had to say. Not so. My highest hope is that when I get through with these remarks, he will rise and say, "Yes, those were exactly the points that I wanted to make." Some of these topics can easily be misinterpreted, and a sharpening of positions is called for.

There are three broad topics that can be raised for separate consideration. One is the conception derived from the Carroll time-to-mastery model. The second is what we have called at Stanford the aptitude-treatment interaction problem — the idea that we should be concerned with designing different methods of instruction as our way of handling individual differences, rather than concentrating only on differences in what the person is expected to learn or differences in pacing. And the third is the comments on measurement and evaluation.

The measurement matter pervades the paper, because Dr. Bloom has accepted a view, increasingly voiced by specialists in measurement, that the psychologists have perverted educational measurement with their emphasis on individual differences and that only attention to the absolute — What does the pupil know? What level of development has been reached in this, that and the other respect? — says anything significant to the educator. The issue has been stated well in Bloom's paper and I shall not elaborate on it. I shall quibble with one point. I would hope that the use of tests for monitoring purposes, for keeping track of the individual learner, will be called "monitoring evaluation" or something else. Mike Scriven and I have had a good dialogue going with a quite different meaning for the word "formative," and it is not going to help Mike and me convert the world if Ben takes the word over for something logically different.

Concerning the aptitude-treatment interaction, I must again be brief. As Ben said, Professor Snow and I have just completed a fairly massive survey of all the literature we could get into a much-too-hurried technical report we were required to deliver. While the dust hasn't yet settled from our scurrying through archives and privately distributed reports, I, at least, find the picture quite distressing. I truly believe that pupils have different ways of learning, that there should be different ways of instructing them in the same subject matter, and that we should be able then to design instruction that in subtle ways changes the approach to fit different pupils. It is a fair summary of our search to say that there is no cross-validated result of an aptitude-treatment interaction.

Interactions do appear, though there are also plenty of studies that claim interaction which, when properly analyzed, show none. Some studies that do show interactions have analyzed them in such a complex way that the results are misinterpreted. The results are inconsistent. At this point we are limited almost entirely to studies that deal, not with the messy classroom situation where there are new lessons each day, but with laboratory paired-associate lists and the like where the stimulus is the same throughout the learning period. We do not have studies which continued long enough to look at the learning-to-learn phenomenon — the student's ability to take advantage of a new method of teaching. A method that looks bad in the first forty minutes of experimentation may turn out to be a good one for some pupils after they get the hang of it. So, the state of the art in this field is very primitive.

On the other hand, there are some indications that we should be able to nail down solid results in the next ten years. In the first place, Herbert Woodrow was mistaken in challenging psychologists who had said that intelligence is the ability to learn. He thought that there is a zero correlation between intelligence, however you measure it, and the ability to learn. That is not supported by the literature. Conventional mental tests are consistently correlated with the student's ability to learn material having no prerequisites, material that stands on its own feet. It is true, as Arthur Jensen has said, that rote learning stands off separately; there may be places, then, where a person who is not good in what we conventionally call general mental ability will be able to make more rapid progress through rote learning. This is one hint at an interaction, but one that is going to be perilously limited for educational purposes. Not much of what I want the school to teach can be taught by rote.

We find numerous instances of interaction of one further kind. In these, one method of teaching is rather strongly correlated with conventional mental tests, so that the pupils that the teacher calls bright do learn faster, and some alternative method of instruction used in the experiment has a much lower, sometimes a zero or negative correlation. Insofar as I can characterize the findings in these heterogeneous studies, it seems that the bright student profits when he is asked to organize, is able to supply meanings, is given some freedom to work on the material and make sense of it. He is better able to profit from verbal semantic training — verbal learning where the materials have implicit meanings that he can work out. There is much less dependence on conventional aptitude when the meanings are painstakingly supplied by text or teacher. This, you might think, would be good for everyone, but the evidence suggests that spoon-feeding the meaning can be detrimental to the superior student. (Where there is no meaning to be found, where the material is strictly meaningless, the conventional aptitude seems to be irrelevant.)

My estimate that it will take ten years of research to bring effects like this under control, so that we will have some understanding of the relation of aptitude and learning, is perhaps an optimistic one. Until now we have shared the hope expressed in Professor Bloom's paper, that the Thurstone-Guilford types of aptitude will open up a number of instructional possibilities. Apparently not, as the evidence now stands. The published studies of that sort either have not succeeded in detecting any relation, such as that between spatial abilities and figural treatment, or they have dealt with complex non-reproducible instructional situations and so are essentially nothing but anecdotal reports. Obviously, this is not a criticism of the Venn-diagram story Ben told you; I have not seen those data and am in no position to evaluate that particular study. I am talking about the literature we have searched rather painstakingly and about one frustrating experience Nancy Hamilton Markle had here, trying to do precisely what Ben called for, that is, develop a treatment that would capitalize on spatial ability.

Let us move on to the matter of mastery, because that is the important theme. This slogan can easily raise echoes of the educational philosophy we used to call essentialism. It seems to echo the Council on Basic Education theme: "Let's get tough and not let anyone have a high school diploma until he has mastered the common branches." It lies in the tradition of Skinner and Glaser and Gagné, who are excellent and useful psychologists but are committed to a rather narrow view that limits education to training.

A great deal of writing forces us to bring to consciousness this dichotomy between training and educational development and take it quite seriously, and to decide how these two modes of instruction can be used. They do different things. Psychologists writing on education are often prepared to say that the whole of schooling is training because that is what current psychological theory can handle nicely. I find the concept of mastery severely limiting, and in trying to find out where my distress lies, I finally focused on one word in the Bloom paper: he states that mastery learning is most appropriate, most practical where the subject matter is *closed*. Training is closed. In a training program you know just what you want the person to do. You know what the stimuli will be, you know exactly the motions the man is to go through or the responses that society has approved, whether in the school or in business or in the military. In education the problems are open. We are preparing people for a world where we do not know the stimuli to be encountered or the responses to be desired, but we have some agreement on the criteria that mark desirable responses.

Bloom makes a number of statements implying a closed model of instruction. We have to get the pupil to master what the teacher has to teach, he says — but the teacher has it in his power to teach *more* than he, the teacher, knows. The pupil has to be equipped to deal with a world the teacher hasn't lived in. To stipulate that the teacher has a limited set of formulas to pass on is to retreat from the problems of instruction that perplex and interest me.

I see educational development as continuous and open-ended. "Mastery" seems to imply that at some point we get to the end of what is to be taught. When Ben ran into this problem, he dodged it, I think. At one point, for instance, he talked about citizenship education which certainly has this continuous and open-ended character, and his retreat was to introduce the phrase "limited degrees of mastery." The iron law, "We are going to bring pupils up to mastery," is vitiated by saying "and we will settle for limited degrees of it." This at least has to be explicated enough that we understand that qualifying phrase. Perhaps, where common sense forces us to invoke the qualifier, the advocate of "mastery" has no message for the educator.

I question that what is to be learned can be identified with a performance criterion. Some writers — but possibly not Professor Bloom — do believe that the end of learning is performance and that the performance criterion tells you whether the pupil has gotten to mastery. But even a well-developed performance criterion leaves open the possibility that the person who showed "mastery" may have poor retention, or poor transfer, or poor ability to maintain this skill or knowledge under stress and confusion. In other words, the concept that we can bring people to 100-per-cent performance is extremely deceptive. People have been trained to *perform* to criterion on the pursuit rotor, for instance — to keep that little stylus right on the revolving dime and never let it slip off. When the experimenter measures again after some time, or after introducing distraction or fatigue, the skill falls apart in some people, whereas in others it stays. Obviously, despite the perfect scores, there were differences in degrees of mastery. We have to talk about development along a scale, and not pretend as we do in the usual definition of mastery that a high score implies an established, perfect performance.

The performance criterion is likely to take the product and not the process as the target. You can bring people to performance of a specified sort in a variety of different ways, and some people may be learning unwanted processes. There's the lovely little experiment of Smedslund's. You will recall that he was trying to train children in conservation of weight. He could train them beautifully; the only catch was that they didn't really believe the concept. They could give the right response to all the regular problems, but when he challenged the answers by a little counterpropaganda the pupils went right along with the counterpropaganda. Learning to reject future counterarguments — whatever they may be — is a very different sort of learning from arriving at 100-per-cent performance on the problem in the textbook.

I was once enthusiastic about the Carroll model. The Carroll paper is a good paper and I thought it was moving us in a worthwhile direction. But as we tried to work with this idea in our research, we abandoned it. We abandoned the whole notion of time to mastery or time to reach criterion or rate of learning. Why? Because learning is multi-dimensional. It is multi-dimensional in a laboratory; it is far more multi-dimensional in the school. As we are teaching one thing, a lot of additional things are happening. The point is implicit in Dr. Bloom's paper. But mastery of what? If the mastery is of the facts of history, is it also mastery of reading historical documents, of a sane attitude toward authority, of pride in one's antecedents, of a sense of the possibilities of social change, and all the other outcomes we think desirable? Even in the subjects at the center of the curriculum, such as reading comprehension, achievement is multi-dimensional. There is the level of knowing what the author said, the level of knowing what the author meant, and the level of understanding things the author said that the author wasn't aware he had said. These aspects of reading comprehension are developed continuously and the child who has been "brought up to mastery" on only one of the dimensions probably hasn't mastered the other dimensions. Nor does the teacher know what to do to cause him to "master" reading in all these ways. The teacher can only hope that repeated interactions with material, discussed at whatever level the pupil *can* discuss these less obvious meanings, will successively move the child along. This is what we speak of as growth or educational development, and I, at least, have not been able to apply the mastery concept to it.

The things for which we can clearly use a training methodology designed to bring people to a performance criterion apparently are limited to static knowledge and algorithms. Much learning of that kind will be useful within the pupil's lifetime, but basically, these skills constitute education for a static society. To get the educated person we need, we are going to have to have a three-stage rocket. The first-stage rocket is training. The training orientation produces trained responses, shapes the behavior we want in some basic and essential areas. But even here I note that Carl Bereiter, who is using a training methodology for pre-school children, warns pessimistically that when you teach a tool you can teach it so that the intelligent and the unintelligent both learn it, but the intelligent, having mastered the tool, will use it intelligently and the unintelligent will use it unintelligently. The second-stage rocket brings the person to intelligent analysis and problem-solving. And the third one goes beyond that to foster creative, self-expressive production. While I accept much that Dr. Bloom has said about the first stage, I think that a straight-line curriculum pointing directly at the training target will miss the second- and third-stage outcomes.

I end by reminding you of a proverb Martin Mayer used at one point which deserves a place in curriculum theory. This French proverb has nothing to do with mastery learning, but then Ben has already told us the French don't understand this point of view. As the French wisdom has it, "One's education is complete when he has forgotten the *lessons* learned in school."

*On a terminé son education ... ...
... qu'il a appris tie.*

*On termine son education quand il oublie
tous qu'il apprendait.*

*L'education est terminé quand on oublie
tous qu'il apprendait.*

*L'education est terminé quand on oublie
toutes les leçon qu'il apprendait.*

TWO

ROBERT KARPLUS

SOME THOUGHTS ON SCIENCE CURRICULUM DEVELOPMENT

My remarks will be quite frank, somewhat personal, and I hope provocative. They do not reflect the official position of the Science Curriculum Improvement Study (SCIS), where most of my experience has been gained.

As a relatively recent newcomer to the field of education, I am not committed to any particular theory in the social sciences. In fact, I believe that there is no satisfactory theory of instruction or of learning which leads unambiguously to a teaching-learning experience once an educational objective has been specified. Instead, there are fragments of theories dealing with parts, and often quite small parts, of the whole picture. My approach to questions or decisions in curriculum construction has been to rely on the judgment (or "hunches") of my colleagues and myself, and to subject this judgment to empirical tests in elementary school classrooms or other appropriate teaching situations. After this test, it has almost always been possible to "explain" the result on the basis of one theory and to use it to show the inadequacy of other theories. Unfortunately, we were usually not able to identify the appropriate theory and its specific form of application in advance. Yet, to be a genuinely useful tool, a theory must be employed in advance, and should reduce the need for experimental testing of teaching hypotheses.[1]

What are some decisions that have to be made, or questions

56

that have to be answered? Some deal with concepts: Can children learn to use the interaction concept, or the state of a system concept? Some deal with sequence: What difference does it make if the systems concept is taught before or after the interaction concept? Some deal with children's dexterity: Can children operate the alligator clips or Fahnstock clips used to make electrical connections? Some deal with equipment utilization: Can two children work while sharing one relief map, or should each one work with his own map? Some deal with pacing: Should an idea be repeated in several very similar versions, or should more contrasting examples be used in close succession?

I am sure that these questions should be answered differently for different teachers and different groups of children. This fact points up the uniqueness of each school classroom, and the strong dependence of education on the personalities of teacher and children. In utopia each class group would create its own unique curriculum, using the resources of its members, its community, and its natural environment. (According to many of my informed friends, the British infant schools are moving in this direction.) Nevertheless, it is the curriculum developer's responsibility to identify common needs of all classes and to create curriculum materials that can add to the resources available for each class. A large-scale demand for such materials then makes it feasible to produce and market them economically.

In a sense, I have now put myself into the position of defending the existence of the curriculum developer. My basic assumption is that there is value in the specialization of labor here as in other endeavors. With a small number of individuals concentrating their efforts on the solution of common problems, the satisfaction of common needs, and the realization of common opportunities, a large number of teachers will be able to conduct more effective teaching programs.

We can now return to the questions I raised before. In spite of the uniqueness of each classroom, I believe it is important that broadly applicable answers be formulated and made available to teachers. These answers should not be interpreted as unfailing prescriptions for "success," but as a first approximation on which each individual class can improve according to its particular circumstances. I have spent much time on this point because I consider the problem of reconciling the large-scale use of common materials with the unique nature of each class group to be central to the improvement of education. (The problem is analogous to the one faced by the teacher with a program for the whole class and thirty unique children.) I am strongly opposed to the educational philosophy according to which a curriculum developer should establish objectives to be achieved by all children if the teacher uses the materials "correctly." Instead, a range of attainable objectives should be indicated, with the teacher (and children?) imposing his priorities and accordingly choosing or emphasizing activities that can be carried out with the materials. Such an approach provides for variations in the sharing of curriculum responsibility. The new teacher can minimize his contribution by following the suggested outline very closely, while the experienced teacher may adapt the program very extensively to the needs and special interests of his class. It is important, however, that all teachers feel some responsibility for decision-making and do not teach merely "because the book said so."

Now I shall identify several educational principles which I have found quite widely applicable, although they don't come close to forming a comprehensive theory.

1. The program must provide for educational input to the children. This can come from structured experiments, the teacher, reading materials, or other sources. The input is organized into a coherent conceptual structure.

2. The program must provide for spontaneous or autonomous activities by the children which are built on the intrinsic interest of the curriculum materials.

3. Beyond a certain point, educational input is not intrinsically interesting and should be supported by social influences. One of these is the educational or social value of the study, a second is identification with the teacher as model, a third (much less desirable, in my view) is compliance with an authoritarian teacher.

4. The pattern of exploration — invention — discovery[2] provides for alternation of input activities (invention) and more or less spontaneous investigation (exploration, discovery). The autonomous activities, furthermore, provide feedback to aid the teacher in planning continuation of the program.

5. Developmental learning theory is more reliable in the cognitive area; behavioristic learning theory is more appropriate for

attitude formation. One implication of this principle is that concept formation should be pursued at low pressure over long periods of time; that is why individual activities have to fit an overall conceptual structure, but repetition and drill should be minimized. A second implication is that positive attitudes (interest, imaginative proposals, evaluation of ideas) should be encouraged by prompt reinforcement without regard to their level of sophistication or accuracy.

6. Teachers should allow substantial time for pupil talk during a discussion and should not control its flow by channeling all remarks through themselves.

These principles, coupled with the empirical approach of testing all materials with children and/or teachers, have enabled my colleagues and me to cope with our curriculum development problems. Any success we have had in this activity is due to the competence and creative imaginations of the members of the innovative team whose special qualifications complement one another effectively.

There are many organizational details to be provided for in a curriculum development project, and all require attention, care, and effort. Support money must be secured, laboratory schools must be available, teacher education must be provided, equipment must be designed and manufactured, books must be written, illustrated, and printed, information must be furnished to the public, and all the staff members must find satisfaction in their work. For a curriculum project to have a significant impact on the schools, its products must become commercially available. That means identifying and licensing a competent publisher and manufacturer, maintaining quality control checks over their production, supervising their costs and production schedules, acting as intermediary to provide customer service in case of delivery problems, etc. Finally, the new materials must find acceptance in the schools. Even though these matters are not usually considered academic in nature, they are a vital part of the process of affecting education practice and as such are inextricably linked with the curriculum development. It goes without saying that a full-time, carefully selected staff is a *sine qua non*.

The payoff of curriculum development is seen in what happens to teachers and children in the classroom. Curriculum evaluation is concerned with describing the result. I should point out that such an investigation is different from the gathering of feedback that is an essential part of the development process described above. In other words, the classroom testing of trial materials requires the collection of information (feedback) with the help of which the development process can be maintained, adjusted, or reoriented, as necessary. All projects have done this with the help of feedback conferences, teacher questionnaires, classroom observations, and tests of individual children. In curriculum evaluation, by contrast, I refer to the study of what happens in schools which use the new materials. The booklet *What Is Curriculum Evaluation* illustrates the range of activities in which the Science Curriculum Improvement Study has engaged.[3]

Curriculum evaluation is an extended activity of broad scope, because the adoption of a new curriculum, such as "Science — A Process Approach," the new math, or SCIS, has extensive ramifications. First of all, the study has to take place at a time when the materials are stable, that is, not subject to frequent revision and change. Second, it has to last long enough so that some of the longitudinal implications can be examined. Third, it has to deal with single children, classroom groups of children and teachers (including the effects on non-science teaching procedures), entire schools with their teachers and administrators, school district officials who are involved in the teacher education and procurement aspects, and the community which provides financial support and presumably expects certain educational benefits. Unfortunately, the tradition of educational evaluation has concentrated heavily on the achievement of the individual child, and almost no attention has been paid to the objectives for which the teachers actually use curriculum materials or the classroom processes through which teachers try to attain these objectives. No new curriculum has been evaluated definitively from this point of view to my knowledge, though the School Mathematics Study Group has carried out an extensive longitudinal study.

Because the new elementary science materials are only now reaching the public in their final forms, the evaluation I have described is yet to come. I hope someone will undertake such a project, and we should certainly be delighted to cooperate fully. Yet I wonder, is this really part of curriculum development or is this a separate problem?

The time required for implementation of the new science programs will, I hope, result in a moratorium on additional massive projects until the present generation of projects has been digested. I see this time being used for research on children's learning under the conditions of the new programs. It is especially important to bring our knowledge of children's intellectual development in the upper elementary grades to the same level as our knowledge of children in the primary grades. In Piaget's terms, the former covers the transition to formal thought, the latter the transition to concrete operations. The relation of science to mathematics is important, as is the impact of the new linguistic programs on children's ability to act when given written instructions.

Beyond this, I expect a more integrated attack on pre-college science, in contrast to the past decade's separate approach to elementary school, junior high school, and high school. And yet, the undertaking is so massive that I question whether satisfactory leadership can be provided for such a project. I also expect a trend toward inter-disciplinary science at the high school level, with some projects (Portland State) already active. Finally, progress has to be made toward more self-direction by the students. Actually, I am so deeply involved in my present work that I have difficulty speculating further about the future.

REFERENCES

1 See Robert Karplus and Herbert D. Thier, *A New Look at Elementary School Science,* Chicago: Rand McNally & Co., 1967, pp. 14–18 for a summary of procedures used by SCIS.

2 See *ibid.,* pp. 40 ff.

3 Robert Karplus (ed.), *What Is Curriculum Evaluation? Six Answers,* Berkeley: Science Curriculum Improvement Study, University of California, 1968.

Robert G. Bridgham

Comments on

SOME THOUGHTS ON SCIENCE
CURRICULUM DEVELOPMENT

In responding to Bob Karplus's paper I'll consider his topics in reverse order: first, what may happen in science curriculum over the next few years, then the problem of curriculum evaluation, and finally the process of curriculum development and the issues raised by large-scale, federally supported curriculum projects. My vantage point is conditioned by sporadic experience as a peripheral participant in the forming of Harvard Project Physics and by the continuing experience of trying to make sense of the outpouring of new science curricula for myself and my students.

Prediction of the future is always risky, but it can be aided by looking at what has occurred in the past. In looking at the science curriculum projects of the past twelve years, one trend seems fairly apparent — the number of options available to fill any particular curriculum "slot" is growing so much that schools must now choose among several nationally devised curricula. Increasingly, choice of materials is *required* within curricula. Curricula are no longer defined exclusively by the student text; in some recent science curricula (Nuffield Chemistry and Physics and the American elementary science curricula, for example) no text is provided by the curriculum designers, but instead the curriculum is described in a rather elaborate teacher's guide. The traditional straight-line sequence is being broken: Harvard Project Physics is designed with the expectation that optional units will be interpolated as desired into the basic six unit sequence; the third stage of the three-stage Nuffield Chemistry curriculum is titled "A Course of Options"; and in the SCIS "Organisms" unit the sequence is expected to be conditional on students' interest in and questions about phenomena.

The design of materials to increase options has noticeable effects on curriculum development: more time is required, larger staffs are needed, and the evaluation of curricula becomes increasingly complicated. The effectiveness of a science curriculum is as much dependent upon the quality of the choices made between curriculum materials as it is on the quality of the materials themselves. Consequently, communication between curriculum designers and teachers is seen as more and more important and the education of teachers to use the new curriculum materials extends the lifetime of curriculum projects well beyond the date when the project materials "go commercial." I suspect that the continuing existence of semi-permanent project groups (seen, for example, in the continuation of the PSSC group under the aegis of EDC or more clearly in the extended lifetime of the BSCS) will become more the rule than the exception.

This situation, then, leads to one prophecy. In science, a substantial part of continued curriculum development is likely to take place in centers established by earlier curriculum groups. These centers will be increasingly concerned with the education of teachers, and the monitoring and evaluation of curriculum effects, in addition to whatever curriculum renovation they sponsor.

That there will be continued curriculum revision in science is, I think, moderately certain. An over-simple review indicates that there have been three waves of curriculum development in science: first the design of subject matter courses in secondary school science, with some carry-over into single-year courses for late junior high school; second, the design of elementary school sequences, just finishing now; and, finally, the design of courses for the junior high school which is in process and will be continuing for some time. The high school courses are no longer sacrosanct "new curricula"; one doesn't have to listen hard at professional meetings to hear grumblings about their shortcomings. Criticism comes in two forms: the courses are too difficult for many students, and the content of the courses is drawn too narrowly — students complain that the courses have little social or cultural relevance. I agree with Bob Karplus when he says that a more integrated attack on the science curriculum is needed, but I doubt that the need for coherence will motivate the next round. If the next round is more coherent than the last, it will be because funding agencies insist on the coherence, not because of a demand from the schools. New work will probably begin on the secondary and junior high curriculum (which is still plastic) as soon as some reasonable schemes for relating the sciences to social and cultural issues are developed.

Unified or inter-disciplinary science courses permit the greater exploration of social and cultural ties, but these ties could also be explicated in a curriculum arrangement in which each of the separate sciences is associated with a particular kind of tie. For example, the use of a developed scientific framework to define societal problems and suggest possible problem solutions might be handled in biology — many biologists are currently occupied with problems of population, pollution, and ecological balance in human environments. In chemistry the interaction of science, technology, and society might be considered, and so on. We will almost certainly have an opportunity to reconsider the shape and flow of the science curriculum, but whether we will seize the opportunity is an open question.

Bob Karplus's idea that important studies in curriculum evaluation will pay special attention to the teacher — what she hopes to do with the curricular materials and how she goes about doing it — deserves some appreciation and elaboration. One characteristic which all the new science curricula have in common is the production of effective and informative guides for teachers. The teacher's guide carries a large part of the burden of communicating the intentions of the curriculum designers to the teacher. It does this, in part, by discussion of these intentions and their relation to course materials, and, in part, by suggesting time allotments, by labeling some laboratory and homework exercises as "essential," by suggesting possible lesson plans, etc. One aspect of curriculum evaluation really ought to be an assessment of the adequacy of this communication. What gets communicated and how?

New curricula can be thought of as trajectories through pedagogic space; they are properly defined not by single lines in that space, but rather by envelopes containing an infinite set of "allowed" solutions to the problems envisaged by the curriculum designers. The problem of curriculum evaluation, it seems to me, is two-fold; to develop means of discriminating teacher trajectories inside the envelope from those outside it, and to determine the effects of trajectories inside the envelope. Of a teacher who has "adopted" a new curriculum we might ask: Is the course of her teaching within the "curriculum envelope"? How does the course of her teaching affect student interaction with curriculum materials, and the range and extent of changes in students — desired and not-desired, anticipated and unanticipated? How do teachers' perception of the curriculum, intentions for the curriculum, and the use of the curriculum materials change from year to year? I have heard it said that teachers tend to rely on the teacher's guide in their first year of teaching a curriculum, to make small departures from suggested procedure in the second year, and to redesign the curriculum in the third year. What forms of intervention are likely to affect this year-to-year change? Curriculum projects, the federal government, and both together sponsor a variety of teacher-education programs. We know very little about their effects.

Careful work which looks at the curriculum-teacher-student triad will require considerable instrumentation not now available. It will not be enough to describe teaching in terms of the general formal categories which currently guide classroom observation, although the instruments which yield these categories may be useful. Observation instruments that are peculiarly suited to a particular curriculum will be essential. Two of our doctoral candidates have worked on observation instruments for particular curricula, and while the going has not been particularly easy, the results are promising. Perhaps the most encouraging aspect of their work is that they were forced to provide observers with curricular materials, in this case student texts, in order to get reasonable observer agreement in the classification of teacher behaviors. Apparently, observation instruments can be developed that are sensitive to curriculum content. But it isn't only teacher behavior that requires careful description; teachers' perceptions of the curriculum designers intentions, as well as their own intentions, go unexamined because we haven't worked out reasonably adequate means for probing them. The development of adequate instrumentation is possible, but only if those who do curriculum research look beyond the constructs and instruments provided them by social psychologists.

While curriculum evaluation has not been as full-bodied as required, one can at least see the skeleton of a more comprehensive effort in the field. However, adequate study of large-scale curriculum development, per se, has not even reached the skeletal stage. If large-scale curriculum development is not going to be a relatively constant feature of the educational scene, no great harm is done by this. But evidence indicates that large-scale projects *will* be around through the foreseeable future. It then makes sense to study the processes of curriculum development, the language used by developers, and the more or less common arrangements found in curriculum development operations. There is undoubtedly a lore of curriculum construction that has developed through contacts at conferences such as this, over cocktails at professional meetings, etc. Many practical, judgmental questions are probably adequately handled through these informal mechanisms. These mechanisms, however, are likely to be inadequate for more penetrating study of the practices of curriculum construction.

As an example, consider what Bob Karplus calls an essential element of curriculum development — the gathering of feedback on curricular materials. After an internal review most projects release materials for use by trial teachers. The teachers are typically asked to comment on the functioning of the materials in their classes: the feedback may come in written responses to a questionnaire, sent periodically to the teachers; it may come orally in scheduled group sessions or in formal or informal individual contacts. The information sought varies from straightforward data (How long? How practical? What errors?) to supported or unsupported inferences (Was there understanding, interest, etc.? Did different types of students react differently? Should the sequence be tinkered with or entirely reworked?). Different teachers will give information of different quality and type: some will focus on particulars, others on inferences from these particulars; some will focus on materials, some on the students' interaction with materials, some on the development of ideas through the materials. Here are a few questions which can motivate study: Can an identification be made beforehand of teachers likely to give one or another form of information? Do different procedures for gathering feedback change the relative amount and quality of different types of information? In the early stages of a project, when many decisions must be made on the basis of information provided by trial teachers, the quality of relevance of this information is crucial. Surely it is important to maximize the value of this information. Systematic and careful study could help, but to my knowledge, there has been little such study.

Curriculum developers are probably not the people to study the processes of curriculum development. Their attention is and ought to be on *what* they are doing, not on *how* they are doing it. Curriculum developers could, however, encourage "outsiders" to study the processes of development and could ensure tolerance of these "unproductive" outsiders by project staff.

Finally, I'd like to highlight Karplus's statement about the centrality of "reconciling large-scale use of common materials with the unique nature of each class group." The tension between a desire for common materials and learnings and the hope of uniquely appropriate learning is found not only in the relation of a widespread curriculum and an individual class, but also in the relation between a class and an individual student. The first form of the tension results from a recognition of the teacher's integrity and abilities, the second from a recognition of the student's integrity and abilities. When a curriculum is adopted by a school we expect that this adoption is a responsible act, that the teachers find the curriculum consistent with their own ends and will work within the curriculum, adjusting it as need be to the particulars of their own unique classrooms. But this adjustment follows from their participation in the choice of a curriculum — a choice of considerable importance. Where in the new elementary science curricula is there an analagous choice for the student? The options provided by the exploration and discovery elements of the SCIS teaching cycle are simply not of this scale. They are, rather, counterparts of the teacher's response, within the chosen curriculum, to his unique setting.

One doesn't have to deny the desirability of common learnings to suggest that students ought to be making major curriculum decisions too. The occasional commitment of large blocks of school time to studies in science chosen by students seems a reasonable way to balance common and unique learnings. The number of options provided need not be large. Teachers will choose between four or five distinguishable curriculum patterns in elementary science; students might be offered an equal number of choices. The possibility of shaping a curriculum with a common developmental core and a complementary set of options is not futuristic. The materials for it are at hand in the sequential curricula developed by the Science Curriculum Improvement Study, the MinneMast program, or Science — A Process Approach, and in the array of discrete units provided by the Elementary Science Study.

Bob Karplus hopes that curriculum development in elementary science will be dormant for a while, so that reasonable evaluation of the programs can be made. I, too, hope that an evaluation of the programs in a relatively pure state will be undertaken. However, each of the programs embodies a conception of the student, of learning, of science that is different and each has a powerful appeal. Acknowledgment of that appeal and of the real differences among the curricula leads me to suggest that each curriculum program has provided a part of what a comprehensive, fully human science curriculum will contain. There is still before us a major task of curriculum development in elementary science, but that task — of fitting the parts together so they complement one another — will, perhaps, be done best by the schools.

THREE

EDWARD G. BEGLE

SMSG:
WHERE WE ARE TODAY

I. HISTORICAL BACKGROUND

Some rather substantial changes have taken place in the elementary and secondary school mathematics programs in this country over the past decade. The School Mathematics Study Group claims a good deal of the responsibility for these changes. However, to put things in perspective, I would like to start by reviewing briefly two topics in the history of mathematics.

We have often been accused of starting a revolution in school mathematics. There has indeed been a revolution in school mathematics, but I can assure you that we did not start it. In fact, there was a revolution in mathematics itself which started well over a century ago. It began with some work by a Norwegian mathematician, Abel, and a French mathematician, Galois. They demonstrated, in some mathematical work they did, that by paying careful attention to the structure of mathematics, the way mathematical ideas fit together, rather than relying on intricate and ingenious computations, it was possible to solve difficult and important mathematical problems that had not hitherto been successfully attacked. The importance of this change of emphasis from ingenious computations to basic concepts and the structure of mathematics gradually became clear. It turned out that a great deal could be done in mathematical research by taking this new point of view. By the end of the nineteenth century, or certainly by the time of the First World War, the nature of mathematics and of mathematical research had completely changed. The mathematics that is done now by research mathematicians is quite unlike the mathematics that was done two centuries ago.

This revolution in mathematics affected mathematical research first. However, it began to penetrate into graduate training in mathematics after the First World War. By the end of the Second World War, these ideas had penetrated down into the undergraduate program, and this emphasis on basic concepts and on structure was found to be powerful not only in mathematical research but also in mathematical education. Much more mathematics could be taught at the undergraduate level, and by the fifties this point of view towards mathematics was generally accepted in the college and university mathematical community.

My second historical topic is, in a slightly negative way, somewhat closer to pre-college education. At the end of the First World War we had in this country a very small number of competent research mathematicians. Some of them were world-renowned, but the community was very small. Throughout the twenties it was not uncommon for students to go abroad for a Ph.D. in mathematics.

These mathematicians decided that it was important to strengthen and increase the size of the mathematical research community here and to attempt to make the United States into a world power in mathematics. It took twenty years, but they succeeded. By the beginning of World War II, the United States was the equal of any other country in the world in mathematical research, and still is.

But in order to carry out this difficult task, the research mathematicians had to devote all possible time to the training of new research mathematicians, the improvement of graduate programs, etc. In particular, no time was available for communication between these mathematical scholars and those concerned with the pre-college mathematics programs, particularly the textbook writers. As a result the curriculum, particularly for the high schools, went gradually downhill and relied more and more on computational tricks and the memorization of a large number of unrelated facts. The unsatisfactory nature of this curriculum was made startlingly clear by the demands during World War II for large numbers of individuals with competence in mathematics, a demand that could not be satisfied.

Thus, by 1950 we had in this country, on the one hand, a large number of very good mathematicians and a modern and effective undergraduate and graduate mathematics program, and on the other hand, an unsatisfactory and ineffective pre-college program and a serious lack of communication between those responsible for this program and the research mathematicians.

At about this time, mathematicians began to think about responsibilities other than that of increasing the United States' research capability. A growing number of very competent mathematicians came to the conclusion that the pre-college mathematics program needed strengthening, and expressed a willingness to provide whatever assistance they could.

Thus, by the time that Sputnik I went up and money became available for large-scale curriculum projects in mathematics, there was a considerable number of mathematical scholars who were interested in pre-college mathematics and there was practically unanimous opinion among them as to how such improvement might be made. Consequently, the School Mathematics Study Group which came into existence early in 1958 was pretty clear about where it wanted to go: to see if it might be possible and helpful to instill into pre-college mathematics some of the spirit and point of view of mathematics itself.

II. BASIC DECISIONS OF THE PROGRAM

Now let me turn to the activities of the School Mathematics Study Group. One of the things that fascinates me as I look back over the past eleven years, is the large number of very basic decisions that the group had to reach and the wide variety of procedures used in reaching them. Some of these seem to have been made by default because no one suggested anything else. One of these decisions is the one mentioned at the end of the preceding paragraph. No one suggested any way of changing secondary school mathematics programs except to increase the emphasis on basic concepts and the way in which they fit together. It is true that there were a few members, mostly applied mathematicians, who made the contrary suggestion that the only way to do mathematics is to start with applications and to build up mathematics just for its applications. However, this group was not listened to.

There had been, and there continued to be, considerable discussion as to why such a change in emphasis would be an improvement for students. The main reason advanced was that it was perfectly clear that the use of mathematics in our society had been growing and would undoubtedly continue to grow at an increasing rate. Not only was more mathematics being used, but it was being used in many more parts of our culture than it was, say, a generation ago. The chance that a student in school, at the time when we started our work, would at some time have to make non-trivial use of mathematics after he left school was considerably larger than it had been in the past. Unfortunately, however, we cannot tell while students are still in school which ones are going to be the users of mathematics later, and hence we felt that we would like to expose students to proper mathematics just on the increasing chance that they would really have to use it later. It was also observed that the uses of mathematics depend as much on the conceptual side as on the computational side and that much mathematics being used a decade ago had only been created within the previous generation. We felt it likely that a considerable number of our students would have to learn within their lifetimes some new mathematics not yet in existence when they were in school, and we felt that having a good understanding of mathematics would make the learning easier than would the mere possession of technical skills.

Thus, this decision was made by default in the sense that no alternatives were seriously considered.

In a case of another early decision, we had plenty of alternatives to think about. Mathematics is taught at every grade level, but it was clear to us that we did not have the manpower to attack the entire curriculum at one fell swoop. We therefore had to decide where we would start working. One alternative would have been to start with grade one and to work up the curriculum. Instead, we decided to start at the high school level and even there to restrict our attention to the mathematics curriculum for college-capable students.

The main reason for this decision was that we had also decided that the communication gap between classroom teachers and university mathematicians had to be bridged and that our efforts at curriculum reform had to be a joint undertaking since each group could contribute something that the other group could not. The classroom teacher did not understand mathematics well enough and college teachers did not understand high school teaching and students well enough. We decided, therefore, to start where the differences were smallest. The college-capable high school student is more like the university student than elementary or junior high school students are, and high school mathematics teachers have a better mathematics training than do teachers at lower grades.

I might say that we also decided that as soon as we got well started on our work at one level, we would move down to the next lower level and work there. By the end of our work we had indeed covered the entire pre-university mathematics curriculum.

Another decision which we made early is that we would try to do something that could be used fairly widely and fairly quickly. This meant that we would not try to make radical changes in the curriculum, and in fact, we set for ourselves the goal of making changes which a teacher could adapt to with one summer institute or one academic year of in-service training. This decision also persuaded us that we should, at least at the beginning, not try to modify the normal placement of topics.

Next we had to decide what we could do that would result in actual changes in the classrooms in this country. We were quite convinced that merely preparing detailed syllabuses and delivering sermons about the virtues of our conception of mathematics would have little effect. We came to the conclusion that it was necessary to provide classroom teachers with actual textbooks in which mathematics was developed from our point of view, that without the support of such textbooks teachers would find it very difficult to make any changes. And this is what we did.

Some later decisions were developed out of and based on our early experiences. When preliminary versions of our first textbooks were ready, we located a number of school systems, scattered around the country, in each of which half a dozen teachers tried the text in class. We found that these tryout centers constituted an effective two-way information network. Other teachers in these school systems and in neighboring school systems were finding out about our work, and we were getting useful feedback about the effectiveness of our texts and the interest which they were arousing. As other textbooks were prepared, the same tryout center procedure was used, and we took care to get a good geographical distribution of them.

The first versions of our textbooks were paperbacks, produced by photo-offset from a typewritten manuscript. These of course were considerably cheaper than a hard-cover letterpress version would have been, but we found that both students and teachers were perfectly happy with our versions, while the lower price made it easier for schools to experiment with our materials. Consequently, we are still producing only the inexpensive paperback version.

I mentioned earlier that our first target was the college-capable high school student. We felt however that the material in the next texts we produced, those for junior high school, were probably suitable for a wider ability range. We were encouraged in this belief by many reports from the tryout classrooms. We therefore prepared alternate versions in which the reading level was lowered and the material presented in smaller chunks and shorter chapters. These proved to be quite satisfactory for students in the 25th to 50th percentile on ability and we came to the decision that we should continue to seek ways to make mathematical ideas accessible to the less able students. We have done some work with disadvantaged children at the primary level and some other work with very low achieving junior high school students and continue to believe that this decision was wise.

This is enough, I believe, to illustrate the fact that our basic decisions, which of course constitute our general philosophy, were arrived at in a variety of ways. Certainly our basic philosophy was not fully and explicitly formed when we started.

III. ORGANIZATION OF PLANNING GROUPS

Let me turn now to some comments on our methods of operation since some of the lessons we have learned may be useful to others engaged in curriculum construction. When we decided to write a textbook, our first step was to organize a planning group. The size of the group varied considerably from case to case, but averaged around ten. These groups were divided equally between classroom teachers and research mathematicians, although occasionally an educational expert or a scientist or an engineer would be included. Each group met for anywhere from one to four weeks to prepare a fairly detailed outline of the text. Sometimes these planning sessions were held during the summer and sometimes during the academic year.

Until quite recently, the actual writing of the first draft of a text would be done during the summer during a six-to-eight-week writing session. The summer was chosen because only at that time could a large and varied group of writers be brought together.

These summer writing teams again varied in size but the average was somewhere between fifteen and twenty, and of course each writing team contained a substantial representation from the outlining team. Again, there was an equal division between research mathematicians and classroom teachers. We found that with a group of about fifteen writers, we could prepare a preliminary version of a textbook intended for use during a full academic year and at the same time prepare a rather extensive commentary for the teachers. These commentaries were generally thicker than the student text because we wanted to make available to the teachers not only any ideas we had for teaching the material but also some extra mathematical background which they might not have had.

These preliminary versions were then tried out in a number of classes, as mentioned above, during the academic year immediately following the summer. From these tryouts we got back considerable information from the teachers through questionnaires. The chief thing we wanted to find out from these tryouts was whether the teachers felt comfortable with the material and whether they felt that they could handle it in their classes. The feedback from the teachers on the student text and the teacher's commentary were both used during the following summer when a revision of the preliminary version was prepared. The writing team for the revision usually consisted of a substantial fraction of the original writing team. Very seldom were any new writers added at this stage. In some cases one revision was thought to be enough for our purposes, but in a few cases we went through this tryout-and-revision cycle twice.

We had some variations in the way we got feedback from the teachers. We started out by merely using questionnaires. We found later that a very valuable supplement was to bring together a random sample of the tryout teachers for a one-or-two-day discussion with the writing team. Also, some of the classroom teachers who participated in the writing also served as tryout teachers and brought back their experiences directly to the revision team.

The tryouts were spread pretty widely across the country, so we did very little in the way of systematic observation in the classrooms, although we did get some anecdotal reports from the mathematicians in the tryout centers who provided in-service training to the teachers, and these reports were sometimes helpful.

We learned by experience that the size of a writing team is quite important, and in fact, that about fifteen is optimal. We have tried larger groups with more than twenty members. These turned out to be too big for efficient communication and discussion. We considered discussion very important. Our general procedure was to parcel out the various chapters of a text to individual members of the writing team for the preparation of first drafts. Each of these drafts was reproduced and distributed to the entire team. These drafts were then discussed and criticized in detail, again by the entire team. Revisions were then prepared, taking into account the discussion and criticism, and the process was repeated until substantial agreement was reached. A team of twenty or more individuals was too large for effective discussion.

We also found that small writing teams, of fewer than ten members, were even less satisfactory. The reason for this seems to be that in a small group individual idiosyncrasies are not as easily spotted during group discussions as in a larger group and wild ideas that look good at first glance are too likely to slip through without elimination. Also a small group does not provide as many good new ideas as does a larger group.

IV. PREPARATION OF TEXTS

Using these procedures we were able, in a little over a decade, to produce at least one textbook for each grade level from nursery school through grade twelve. Of course for the nursery school and kindergarten there is merely a book for the teacher and no written material for the students. Our original thought was that one textbook per grade level would be sufficient to provide a concrete example of the kind of curriculum that we thought both feasible and appropriate for today's children. We hoped that these texts would provide guidance and suggestions for the authors of a wide variety of commercial texts at each level.

However, as time went on we found it desirable to write additional texts at certain levels. There were a number of reasons for this. For example, there is still a good deal of controversy among mathematicians as to how geometry should be treated in the high school. There are some who feel that a cleaned-up version of the traditional Euclidean approach would be best, but others argue for a variety of other approaches. We therefore wrote a second tenth-grade geometry text utilizing one of the other approaches to geometry.

Also, at the beginning of this decade some pretty wild claims were being made for programmed learning and some of the programmed mathematics texts that were appearing looked pretty bad to us. We therefore undertook to find out if it was actually possible to program a full year's course of mathematics of the kind we were trying to emphasize. We prepared a programmed version of our ninth-grade algebra text. It turned out to be considerably more time-consuming to prepare than the original text. I might say that we found that students did learn algebra just about as well from the programmed text as from the original version, but many of them were quite bored by programmed material, and we found very few teachers who enjoyed using it.

There were some topics which we had not originally considered for inclusion in the pre-university curriculum. As time went on we found that we had to change our minds about some of these. In particular, it became clear that probability and statistics were playing a very important role in our culture and that an introduction to the basic ideas of probability ought to be made available to all students. We therefore prepared some short elementary and junior high school units on probability which turned out to be quite effective. We are all aware of the increasing impact of high-speed computers on our culture. Because of this, we ended up by preparing a senior-level mathematics course devoted to algorithmic aspects of mathematics. The purpose of this text was not to make expert programmers out of the students, but rather to give them a better understanding than most people have as to what computers can do and also what they cannot do.

I have already mentioned that we prepared special versions of our junior high school texts aimed at slower students. We also prepared modifications of our kindergarten and first-grade materials for use in the slum areas of the big cities. These were based on a two-year observation program of kindergarten and first-grade classes.

In addition to these texts and the accompanying teacher's commentaries, we have also put out a number of supporting series of publications. We have a series of books intended explicitly for the in-service training of teachers. We have a series of monographs intended for supplementary reading, especially by the more interested and more able students. We have translated a number of our texts into Spanish for use in Puerto Rico.

In the preparation of these materials, as was the case with the preparation of texts for students, everything that was done was a joint effort of the mathematical scholars and the classroom teachers. It has been a great joy to me to see that this has worked so well and to see how each group has realized what sort of contributions it can make and how important the contributions from the other group are. One of the most important by-products of our work has been that we have now trained a very large number of university mathematicians in working with elementary or secondary school teachers and in writing text materials. The commercial texts that are now coming out, as we had hoped would be the case, are going along the lines that we originally suggested and are being written in part by some very good research mathematicians.

V. EVALUATION OF PROGRAM

Let me now turn to the matter of evaluation. As I mentioned above, our first kind of evaluation was with respect to the classroom teachers. We tried to find out, through questionnaires and interviews, whether the teachers thought that our materials were teachable and how comfortable they felt in using them in actual classroom teaching. Once we were satisfied that we were on the right track in this respect, we began to ask what effect we were having on students. For this purpose we turned to the Educational Testing Service and asked them to compare our textbooks for grades seven, nine, ten, eleven, and twelve with conventional texts for the same grades. (We had not yet finished the eighth-grade text.)

In this carefully designed evaluation, which was carried out in the 1960-61 academic year, student achievement was assessed in two ways. First a standard test, designed for a conventional curriculum, was administered at the end of the year. In addition another test was administered which was designed to cover topics which we had built into our materials but which did not appear in conventional texts. It turned out that students using our texts did, in some cases, about the same on conventional tests as students using conventional texts and in other cases slightly less well. On the other hand, students using our texts did considerably better than the other students on the special tests. This was enough to demonstrate that our texts had done the students no harm, and that we had gotten across some of the new ideas built into our texts. Unfortunately, this was all that we could learn from this evaluation. It gave us no indication as to what we ought to do next. It gave us no indication as to how much value there was in these new things that we were getting across to the students. We therefore decided to undertake a much more elaborate evaluation program.

In the fall of 1962 we began a five-year longitudinal study of mathematics achievement. We started with approximately 35,000 fourth-grade students, 45,000 seventh-grade students, and 30,000 tenth-grade students. These students were located in over forty different states, and the schools in which they were located were using a variety of textbooks — some conventional and some modern. We were interested in finding out what happened under actual rather than artificial circumstances, so we put no restrictions on the schools on curriculum choice, and they were quite free to change curricula if they wished.

Our plan was to assess mathematics achievement each fall and each spring for a period of five years (three years for the tenth-grade students). It was our belief from the beginning that mathematics achievement is multi-variate and cannot be described by a single score. We constructed a two-dimensional array of mathematical objectives. One dimension is specified by mathematical topics: arithmetic, algebraic, geometric, analytic, etc. The other dimension is specified by cognitive level. We chose four levels: computation, comprehension, application, and analysis. Our choice of these four levels was obviously heavily influenced by a study of Bloom's *Taxonomy of Educational Objectives.*

We administered a two-or-three-hour battery of tests in the fall and in the spring of each year. We also collected a great deal of other information through questionnaires of one sort or another, including information about the schools, about the communities in which they were located, about the students (such as age, occupation of parents, number of siblings), and about these students' teachers. We obtained the usual sort of background information about teachers, such as years of teaching experience, highest degree, recency of in-service study, etc. We also administered a rather extensive attitude inventory measuring various teacher attitudes towards teaching, towards students, and towards mathematics.

In the battery we administered to the students were included not only a variety of mathematics scales, constructed to measure student achievement in a number of different cells in the two-dimensional array of mathematical objectives, but also a large variety of psychological tests, both cognitive and affective. At the end of five years we had lost a considerable number of students from the study through normal attrition processes, mainly because the students' parents had moved. Nevertheless, we still had a substantial number of students left for whom we had a large number of mathematics achievement measures and a large number of other measures over a period of years.

The first major analysis that we are carrying out using these data is an attempt to find out how much effect the textbook itself has on student achievement in mathematics over and above the many other measures that we have accumulated. For grades four, five, and six we separated out those students who had used the same textbook sequence for the full three years. We found that we had six textbook sequences for which there were enough schools and enough students to be included in the analysis. One of these was the SMSG sequence, two of the others could be labeled modern, and the other three were quite conventional. We could also make an analysis of two-year sequences for grades seven and eight, but for the higher grades we had to analyze one year at a time. In most cases the number of textbooks in each analysis ran somewhere between eight and twelve, including some modern and some conventional.

Because of budgetary problems, this analysis has not gone very quickly and we are not yet finished. Two interesting findings, however, are already quite apparent. The first is that the effect of the textbook becomes less and less as one moves up the grades. The textbook has quite a strong influence on student achievement in the elementary school but by the end of high school this influence has greatly decreased.

The second finding is that the results are far more complex than we had anticipated. You will remember that we administered a number of different mathematics scales in each test battery. There are large differences in achievement on these different scales both within textbooks or textbook sequences and between them. Profiles of student achievement are quite jagged and quite dissimilar. Our belief in the multi-variate nature of mathematics achievement is completely vindicated.

There are many other analyses which we plan to carry out using these data. For example, we plan to study the effects on mathematics achievement, after initial mathematics achievement and IQ have been partialed out, of each of the many cognitive, affective, demographic, socio-economic, and teacher variables. This should give us a good picture of the relative importance of many of the variables which are suspected of being important in mathematics education. We have already done a pilot study on teacher effectiveness. Using a very large number of students, we are able to compute from beginning-of-the-year scores an expected score for the end of the year on a particular mathematics scale. For a given teacher, the average deviation of his student's actual scores from the predicted scores is a measure of the teacher's "effectiveness." For seventh-grade teachers using a modern textbook we found that there was quite a variation among teachers in their effectiveness as thus defined. The distressing thing is that all the background information we had on these teachers and on their attitudes towards mathematics, teaching, students, etc., accounts for only a few per cent of the variance in the teacher effectiveness scores.

These are examples of the kinds of analyses of our data that we can carry out. There are undoubtedly many others that we will eventually carry out which should prove helpful to school administrators or curriculum developers or researchers in mathematics education.

VI. CURRENT CURRICULUM PLANS

Finally, let me make a few comments about our current curriculum development work. We are trying to put together a new curriculum for junior high school starting with grade seven. This differs from our original curriculum in two important ways. In the first place, we are allowing ourselves to ignore the normal grade placement of topics. Instead we are trying to find a more efficient sequence, and in particular we bring in geometric ideas quite early to help illustrate and strengthen arithmetic and algebraic ideas. At the same time we can use arithmetic and algebraic techniques to help develop geometric concepts.

The mathematical topics contained in this sequence consists of those topics, and only those topics, which we believe every student should have a chance to study. This means that certain topics normally taught in grades seven, eight, or nine are not included on the grounds that, in our opinion, they are merely of technical interest to those who will go farther in mathematics and therefore can be safely postponed. It also means that certain topics, such as algorithmic processes and flow charting, probability, and statistics, are included even though they are now normally taught much later or else to a limited group of students.

This time we are spelling out our objectives a little more completely. I am insisting that the writers provide for each chapter a rationale for the inclusion of the chapter in our new sequence, an explanation of what it contributes to general education or to the development of later chapters in the sequence.

While we are making these objectives explicit, we cannot of course insist that everyone agree with them. However, we did not develop these objectives without considerable advice from others. By means of letters to the standard mathematical journals and also to *Science,* I informed the mathematical and the scientific communities of our intentions and asked for suggestions. A very large number of suggestion were submitted and were carefully reviewed by the planning team for this project. This team contained not only the usual mixture of mathematical scholars and classroom teachers but also a substantial representation from science, engineering, and business. Consequently we believe that this new project will find wider acceptance than it would have

found had we tried to formulate our objectives without this outside consultation.

VII. CONCLUSION

During the eleven years in which our Study Group has been
working we have made a great deal of progress and have, I am
convinced, substantially raised the quality of mathematics education in this country. However, every step of progress has brought
into view new paths that should be followed. There is much left
for us and for others to do.

Michael Scriven

Comments on

SMSG: WHERE WE ARE TODAY

Everybody else has been making nervous remarks about their
commentators, but if you have to comment on a paper you have
never seen and only heard, you get to be a little nervous about
being a commentator: it's a problem of being able to say anything particularly well considered. Moreover, this was a very
highly descriptive account, not a theoretical account, and to that
extent less easy for a philosopher to provide a response to. I
am just going to make a few remarks that occurred to me while
listening to it, but I begin with the comment that these remarks
will be shorter than this monumental enterprise deserves.

I think that my general reaction as a professional evaluator to
the enterprise would be that by this stage of it the developers
have learned the lessons that most of us have also learned over
the same period. In 1959 I don't think you could be too wise
about some of the points that they now rightly see as being
crucial, and so I don't think there is very much point in crack-
ing wise after the event. It is now clear to me and probably to
all of us that there are several things one should strongly recommend that people not do if they were doing this kind of study.

Perhaps the major flaw was the omission of a really serious attempt at what I've called "formative evaluation." Perhaps I should say a word about what I think that various kinds of evaluation should do, particularly since Robert Karplus was talking about this a little this morning. The function of what he called qualitative evaluation is a feedback function, of course, like formative evaluation, but the trouble with the way that Bob Karplus has that categorized in his own mind is that he sees it as essentially an informal business, when in fact that is much too sloppy a way to treat it.

Formative evaluation certainly has a different role from summative evaluation, the turn-in-the-chips evaluation which, of course, ought to be done as rigorously as possible. But the valve of the formative results, which you're going to throw away rather than publish, depends how *you* change your own plans for the curriculum. Their historical significance is zero. But you can't base your plans on invalid interpretations, so the need for design rigor is just as great here as in summative evaluation. In either case you can use informal — unnormed or nonqualitative — scales or tests. In reading through Bob's little book on approaches to evaluation written by some of the people in his project, we see clearly that the element of informalism which was kicking around there has simply meant that they misinterpreted a good deal of their feedback. Several simple errors of experimental design in that outline arise really because a couple of good teachers or curriculum writers decided they needed some feedback from the students or from the teachers and so they set up a few little questions and then they interpreted them. It is done at the level at which a reasonably good second-year psychology student would do it — a student not so much ignorant of points as just not skilled as an evaluator. For example, the whole contaminated vocabulary fallacy turns up throughout: by using a special sense of a term, you get a big gain on a pre-test post-test comparison but the reason for this gain is not greater insight into the notion of "relative position," for example, but the fact that you have taught them a technical meaning for a word in the ordinary language. So it is an almost completely meaningless gain. You don't know whether you have taught something useful or not; it all depends on evaluations you don't have about the utility of other vocabularies for making the same points, and in particular about whether the points were already known to the students if put in terms of their normal vocabulary. That is a standard type of error in most informal evaluation, and of course, corrupts your decisions about what you are going to do. For one thing, it may make you feel good when it should not — or the reverse may, and frequently does happen. You feel you have not done anything, when in fact a decent job of evaluating would show that you have.

Turning to SMSG, I would say that what Ed had going for him (as did PSSC and several other projects) was a great collaboration between two groups which have not been adequately brought together before, namely, the high school teachers and the research professionals, in this case mathematicians. But no representatives of the other two interested parties in that collaboration were present. The other two interested parties are the kids and the taxpayer. Now, the kids are not always and in all respects good representatives of themselves—it is not good enough just putting a bunch of fourth-graders into a meeting with a bunch of red-hot Ph.D.'s in mathematics and some hardened twenty-year veterans of the ghetto school system. That's what an evaluator is for. You can see his role in one way as the representative of the kids — if he is any good, that is. He is also in some sense the representative of the taxpayer. He is supposed to be standing up and saying, "Look, boy, just remember your roles, just watch out for what they will drive you to — a hybrid curriculum with which the teachers are going to be comfortable and which the research mathematicians are going to think is academically respectable. That's a great hybrid but it is not what you are after. It may be reasonable to argue that they are necessary conditions for a good curriculum but they are not a sufficient condition. The sufficient-condition problem comes out of reconciling those two points of view with the student's and the taxpayer's point of view."

In an extreme case, one problem can be put in this way. The teacher will be happier with materials which keep the kids busy and interested because this reduces classroom management problems. The academic researcher will be happier with concepts which are formally more elegant for him and which are logically well sequenced, so that the development of this material makes good mathematical sense. But what is the relationship of that to proper pedagogical sequencing? You don't know. The classroom teacher knows only about teachability, which tells you nothing about optimal sequencing. It may be that you can perfectly well teach SMSG grade four, and that it is better to teach it than something else that could have been taught, and it is mathematically more respectable than the competition, and that you can then build on it to teach grade five and grade six. But you don't even know whether you should have taught the grade six materials first. Now, of course, in some obvious cases it couldn't possibly be done but the whole literature of research on sequencing is really shaky, as most of you know — without even mentioning the readiness mess. This is one point at which I think the possibility of a radically different curriculum emerges immediately, if we are prepared to re-examine sequencing completely. As Ed has suggested, you can't any longer accept constraints imposed by state boards and keep this program the same across the country. And you can't simply accept the word of the mathematician for what concepts should be placed where. The idea of bringing in the professional mathematician is interesting and potentially valuable, but it isn't automatically a guarantee of improved performance by the kids — even on the tasks that the mathematician thinks are important criteria of performance, which again, is the problem of loaded criteria.

Now, then, we come to the new group of advisers, for the junior high, that Ed was just describing in response to Professor Bloom's request. Who were and who should be the eighteen planners? Who are the consumers of mathematics? They are not or at least not only the business administration people. It will be very important which consumers of mathematics you take and it will be important what status they have in that group and how much gut energy they've got so that they can stand up and listen to a guy with Nobel-prize level qualifications telling them what's what in mathematics and say, "No, it really doesn't sound persuasive." Now it's not easy to do that. These mathematical consumers are snowed by the credentials very easily. But it is terribly important that they not be snowed. Because what's going to happen here is what happened in PSSC evaluation, for example. You discover that if you use your tests you win, if you use their tests it is a draw or they win. That is, the overall evaluation curriculum depends upon the evaluation of the tests, not on the performance of the students on a neutral test. Now, evaluating a test is, roughly speaking, evaluation of goals, and evaluation of goals is dependent on philosophy of education, so we get back to this panel of eighteen which is going to be the ultimate source of the total justification of the project. Are they really strong enough to support a claim that in a particular case the goals they prefer are simply better? If not, one is inadequately prepared for an outcome which is rather probable. With PSSC there was some sense in which, professionally speaking, you could say that the goals were better, that is, regarded by professional physicists as better, but nobody really went into the business of what other sorts of payoff there might be from a physics curriculum and tried to work out how you could establish in an objective and reliable way whether those were present with the specific behavioral objectives in the PSSC curriculum. Well, it would be nice not to have to face that situation too many further times and I think the idea of bringing in the panel to look at what should be in the new one is a good start, but I suspect that if I were thinking about doing a project like this, I would be inclined to do it in a slightly different sequence. I would get the panel in and then write the letter to *Science,* which I think is an example of just exactly the right approach — roughly, don't bitch afterwards, produce the wisdom now. Then you get a good crew to work on a list of goal behaviors from these letters and your resource people. But then I would publish the proposed aims. I wouldn't dream of writing a word until I had published what now looked like the criteria and had gotten the second round of feedback because that would be the point at which that panel can be attacked and needs help. Four years later, five years later, when you have the results, somebody can suddenly look at that panel in retrospect and see that it was loaded in a certain way and the results were kind of disappointing, but kind of what we might have expected. Well, let's not have "might have expected," let's try to expect. This is what I think is a good general principle, to try to publish the design and the criteria, as behaviorally specified as you can in advance, with a big fat footnote saying "I reserve the right to abandon every one of these objectives if they turn out to be a pain in the neck to try to implement or if I discover data pointing the other way but right now here we go with a prima facie outline. This isn't a contract, please don't write to me and tell me that I didn't do what I promised to do because I'm not promising to do anything, I'm just telling you what looks good now. If you've got complaints, now is the time to let them rip."

Let me mention a couple of other things. I would like to hear quite a bit more about the programming enterprise, partly because I'm interested in it myself. They did test to see what the kids learned, and the teachers' feedback was very strongly negative, but it turned out the kids were learning just as much. Now that tells me two things which are very important. One is that, considering the exact words of the teachers' feedback, it is almost certain that their judgment was wrong about what the kids were learning. But suppose the teachers' feedback was restricted so that it merely included statements about how the teachers liked working in this situation. Then what it tells me is that nobody really sweated blood on the problem of how you train teachers to work with and enjoy programs. Here is the same problem which Ed has so thoroughly handled in the general design of the study, the "let's get back in our office and write up a good curriculum, and we'll give it to the teachers and they'll go out into the classroom and use it" syndrome, only this time format is causing trouble. Of course, the teachers resented the new materials and didn't understand them, and we got into the whole in-service training kick which is a tremendous step forward and very sensible. But when you use a new technology like programming, you've got to treat it in the same way. What's the background attitude towards programming? They have heard that it is teacher-proof. They have heard that the classes in Roanoke learned just as much without the teacher as they did when the teacher was present teaching conventionally. It is a terrific threat to them. Of course you expect negative feedback from them; therefore, you've got to have prophylactic treatment. What happened was that with antagonistic, pessimistic teachers you got comparable performance. What might have happened in that situation if you had had carefully trained teachers enthusiastic about programming, which releases them from the drudgery of a lot of homework correcting, etc.? Might we not have had a multiplicative effect? Might we not have speeded up a lot of routine learning or improved the handling of divergencies in skill-acquisition rate amongst the skill-divergent age-grouped class?

I think the other side of this is the question of how the material was programmed — the original nightmare problem. Ed said this was the hardest slice to write. If he had said it was the hardest one to write by a factor of at least a hundred to one, then I would know that he was feeling the same way about it as I do. The crucial issue is how much field-testing went on. You can't write the program on the same time-schedule as you could write the other text, you see, because you have to go through three or more cycles of feedback until you get the error rate down without cheating by changing the quizzes. Now, if you have done all that, it is pretty hard for me to imagine that you won't improve the original written material. The reaction to programming illustrates the faddist tendencies in education so well that one must be very careful about it. You know, something comes on the scene, a bunch of idiots say it's going to cure all known educational diseases, everybody is terribly excited but secretly anxious as all hell because it's going to put them out of business and they have their own thing going. So we do a few tests, tremendous results, but is it the Hawthorne effect? We do a few more. The cheap boys' stuff is now flooding the market with rotten versions; it turns out they don't work so well. Ah! Relief! We can put it away. It was just another fad, so we say. What we've done is to illustrate that we're badly trained because we've been through that routine with at least six different innovations in education since the 1940s. We surely should have learned by now that the usual sequence doesn't tell you whether there was a fundamentally good idea involved. To find out if it was fundamentally a good idea, you wait for all that early days nonsense to drop out so that the Hawthorne effect begins to evaporate and you can begin to get selective again about materials and then you are able to make a serious study of what programming can do for you.

That is just about all that I have to say and I'll conclude with a constructive suggestion. It is terribly important when you start putting money into a large-scale support for curriculum reform that you think very hard about earmarking 5 per cent of the budget for mad money. We have the best of inductive reasons for thinking that a number of projects which are completely dissonant with the current pattern of research will set up the paradigm for the next development of a revolutionary kind in science. And from induction from our past experience we know about the rigidity of our own panels which have all old men who think successfully with the existing paradigm. The proper counter-strategy is to allocate 5 per cent to be distributed not on the basis of the judgment that the project is the best out but on the judgment that it is the *wildest* one proposed by a qualified man. "Qualified" does not mean that you agree with him, it just means that he can do the mathematics. In the same way, I think, with these big curriculum projects, it is pretty important that you be running a tiny little thing on the back burner of the stove in which some nut is writing a program that challenges every assumption that you have on the front burners. I've been involved in medical education lately and what we have on the back burner is the idea that in four summer sessions of six weeks each, taking school children in the summers after the ninth through twelfth grades, we can get them to the point where they could pass a practical test for a GP. By that I do not mean the final examination, in the medical school, 90 per cent of which is irrelevant to being a GP, but I mean that you take a slice of the behavior of a GP, allowing yourself to drop 5 or 10 per cent of his cases which really need technical knowledge, and see whether you can meet his accuracy on the rest on the basis of six months' spaced training. In my view, it is almost certain that you can. At the moment everybody who says, horrified, that it can't be done, and then steps down to look at what could not be done gets very shaken because they begin to think that they probably could have done it. It is the same way here; on the back burner of math projects I think that we need to have some guy that says, "To begin with, I'm going to reverse the order of the guides that came from the group that Ed mentioned." I think that if we work back ruthlessly from the goal, building up the minimum mass of material required, being willing to switch over the whole effort to back-burner projects if necessary, we are going to get through the projects faster and we are going to get to a criterion which will be recognized by good men as more valuable socially, and more interesting intellectually — not more respectable professionally. To identify the intellectual approach with the professional attitude is a complete error. The intellectual approach may be the best one for teaching kids to be auto mechanics. We just have to keep the doors open for these wild ones and one reason is that otherwise you can find yourself $5,000,000 down the drain, six years older, and still not sure if you have something. In this way you cover your bets a little bit.

In general it seems to me that the evaluation project as well as the construction one should cast its net rather wider. The actual payoff for us from SMSG has to be measured in many dimensions other than the performance of the kids. For example, what was the difference in the morale of the teachers that were involved in this? Was there a dramatic long-term attitudinal shift? What was the difference in the atmosphere at the schools because of their being involved in an integrated program? What is the difference in the parental involvement in the homes, etc.? Many factors here are peripheral in one sense but may be highly significant socially when you add them up, all of which I think might add to the performance gains that we may directly identify in SMSG.

FOUR

IRVING KAUFMAN

THE ART
OF CURRICULUM MAKING
IN THE ARTS

The testy, but acutely discerning George Bernard Shaw put it well: "I am simply calling attention to the fact that fine art is the only teacher except torture." The connotations of such an attitude as the basis of education are broad and fanciful indeed. Not the least of the connotations is a view of curriculum which honestly asks that school studies be caught up in questions which the arts always ask such as: Who are we? How do we best realize a significant and satisfying life? How does one celebrate the experience of life? Such questions translated into social values and cultural works need to be directly reflected in the making of curriculum and in the dynamic processes of discovery and learning. However, the maddening time lag of the institutionalized educational process often does not permit a pertinent and truly contemporary expression of needs and attitudes in the classroom. The current interest in the personalist and subjective aspects of life as is evidenced most extremely in the hippie and anti-authoritarian attitudes of students does not find a more reasonable base of examination in the schools today than it does in society at large.

Nor, unfortunately, has a constrained society achieved such a mark of awareness of level of sophistication as to accept Shaw's admonition. Be it because of the vestiges of the Puritan ethic or a genetically ingrained masochism, we retain our little tortures in education. Nevertheless, the powers that be occasionally recognize that the arts are of high personal value to students, that they do enhance the general culture, and that they are possessed of basic educational significance in the growth of intelligence as well as the expansion of the spirit. A need, then, is also acknowledged and supported, albeit grudgingly, to study and experience the arts within a pedagogical context. Consequently, the need extends to developing curricula which would prompt imaginative programs in the schools. I am going to report to you of such an instance.

The Central Atlantic Regional Educational Laboratory (CA-REL) located in Washington, D. C., began an arts and humanities curriculum development program early in 1967. The laboratory initially identified its major area of research as early childhood education. After an analysis of educational needs, the research program in early childhood education accepted as its major focus the development of curriculum in the arts and the humanities. In the final formulation, the arts and humanities were identified for program purposes as the visual arts, dance, drama, literature, and music. Curriculum development was broadly conceived in terms of subject and process concepts, classroom activities, teaching materials, and the evaluation of the whole.

As is frequently the fate with cultural and especially artistic undertakings, either in the larger society or in educational circles, philosophical misunderstanding and fiscal tight-fistedness reinforced the little tortures, and the CAREL arts and humanities program was phased out in May 1969. Unfortunately, the phasing-out process came at a time when the program had finally achieved an initial cohesiveness and direction which promised much for future curriculum development in the arts. There may be some insights to be gained, however, from an examination of the program's premises and procedures.

The rationale of the program stressed the relational qualities and the dynamically functioning values of artistic experience rather than factual information or procedural techniques. It emphasized the open processes and transforming activities of art rather than prescriptive objectives and static skills development. It also voiced a parallel concern for the development of literate, critical sensibilities, recognizing the complementing interaction between expressive, artistic participation and critical aesthetic responsiveness.

Fundamentally, those in the program believed that the arts motivate and shape a personally eloquent existence. They felt that the artistic and aesthetic dimensions of education grow out of such a belief. These dimensions provide a fertile condition for establishing identity and creating convincing meaning for the individual beyond that of a public and coercive culture. Also, the arts in education instruct and vitalize the larger environment of culture so that it remains more attuned to the full range of inherent human needs and potentialities. The arts, in short, are vivid ways of feeling and knowing, establishing their own countless — though perhaps paradoxical — truths. The student encounters the qualities and values of the arts directly as sensory and symbolic forms and cues for creatively constituting a personal ordering of reality; experience is one of intrinsic revelation and imaginative adventure. The experience cannot be passive, or largely denotative and predetermined. Art forces the acknowledgement of the student as *homo gaber,* man the maker. A parallel realization of the rationale was that in "making," whether in studio activities or as appreciative recreation of great art, the student formulates an environment which indeed *becomes* his environment — a personally constructed and thus significant world.

Such considerations of dynamic and subjective nature compel the curriculum maker in the arts toward an open and speculative organization of curriculum elements. This organization does not reject philosophical rigor, but rather encourages it, albeit in the direction of a radical empiricism. Such an approach can lead to many fruitful hypotheses, but never to the constraints of codified theory. The premises and activities out of which the curriculum is designed, however, also require sound artistic and aesthetic support. The CAREL program argued that the philosophical criteria are most adequately met by formulating a suggestive framework in each of the arts. The framework establishes a hypothetical foundation for learning experiences which are concept based but process oriented and experientially open-ended. The concepts are not cognitively fixed assumptions or working propositions based upon the informal backgrounds and sensitive intuitions of the artist curriculum designers. This insures a flexibility of response, hopefully, from individual students and alternative teaching suggestions for differing groups and diverse educational settings.

The CAREL program did accept the premise that the arts offer children direct, natural, and enriched means of knowing themselves and of creating significant meaning for the world about them. It reiterated that all children can find in the arts vivid and enhanced ways of learning, that the arts provide creative and satisfying means of transforming feelings, sensations, and ideas into perceptible yet critically qualitative forms of understanding. The program saw the validity of such understanding as primarily a private experience, insistent upon an individual sense of responsibility for the forms created and insights gained. Thus, there was no "right" answer in art, no public and conventional definition to which the children had to adhere. There was only what was "right" for the child because of his intuitive insights and because of affective necessity. It was felt that only when a child was able to express his own feelings and ideas freely could the pressures and guidance of a critical intelligence be brought to bear upon his experience in the arts. Then there could occur the necessary merging of personal expressiveness and critical judgment. The two together establish a sophisticated awareness in the arts leading to an intelligent but personal sensitivity as well as to the probing of worthwhile questions of personal philosophy.

An authentic realization of such artistic aims in education, the program thought, is achieved when the arts are accepted as inherently sufficient activities, valuable for their own sake, rather than primarily instruments toward other learnings or social ends. This view does not deny the many desirable and adjunctive values animated and substantialized through art, such as personality therapy or enhancement of social studies. It does suggest, however, that the experiences of art are intrinsic, that any secondary benefits flow naturally from a respect for the self-sufficiency of the artistic experience. Otherwise, there are seemingly gratuitous considerations. Thus, art becomes a mere catalyst. Its composed relationships are not formal elements and contents joined out of internal necessity, but merely contrivances for relaying external information. The forms of art in this view do not create and establish any meaningful reality; rather they become props toward fashioning and imposing a traditional or prejudiced view of the world. Such considerations obstruct artistic intelligence and an honest involvement with expressive exploration and discovery and alert responsiveness. This often deflects both the aims of art as well as the instrumental learning that could take place. In short, art for art's sake is really art for people's sake.

Another consideration of the CAREL arts and humanities program was that despite any recognition of the legitimacy of the arts in elementary education, the majority of schools do not support local programs taught by specialists. Whatever the reason for the lack of specially prepared personnel, it is apparent that the classroom teacher provides most of the arts experiences for children. Since it is fair to assume that there is hardly a sophisticated level of awareness and competency in the arts among the general run of elementary school teachers, CAREL accepted the responsibility of building an arts and humanities curriculum for use in the ordinary classroom. It thought that any innovations would also influence the often moribund and popularized programs put into practice by "trained" personnel of even the specialized art disciplines.

To create a negotiable and legitimately artistic curriculum the CAREL staff began a liberal design of curriculum building in the arts to reach a large clientele. The curriculum builders decided they had to attend to three broad areas of criteria. First, the substance and structure of the curriculum development was not to violate or compromise the genuine functions and character of the arts. This stand was largely determined by artists and respected scholarly sources. Second, the child's needs and developmental patterns were to be respected, both generally and, more important, as reflected in individual idiosyncrasy. Theoretical as well as empirical evidence furnished the guidelines for this concern, again dependent upon research and scholarly sources, but also responsive to the insights offered by teachers actually working with children. The third factor insisted upon encouraging independent teaching methods based upon a teacher's own life style as it encounters classroom conditions.

This last factor implies that in arts education the freely determined and exemplary nature of the teaching act is central to significant classroom experiences, determining in large measure the qualitative character of that experience. It also suggests that the curriculum cannot be a contained body of knowledge and procedure given over to the teacher intact. Rather, the supposition is that the act of teaching is an unfinished event until the actual teacher, children, particular situation, and environment are in active relationship. Then, conceivably, with the suggestive assistance rather than prescriptive direction of a curriculum the teacher accepting the dynamics of his role can complete the singu-

larly distinctive act of teaching. Though written materials are
provided, in a very important sense, teachers create their own
curricula, in that what and how they teach comprise the actual or
existential curriculum to which students are exposed. In other
words, at least in arts education, there are no teacher-proof
curricula.

Two final aspects of the rationale are important to mention.
They are, perhaps, the most distinguishing factors of the CAREL
arts and humanities program. One is the need to develop a process
model curriculum in the arts. The other is the acceptance of
practicing and professional artists as curriculum conceptualizers
in each of the designated art fields.

Briefly, the latter aspect endorses the assumption that the committed, mature artist is most likely to have the insights and knowledge concerning various art forms and the capacity to conceptualize their role in education. Working in conjunction with teachers
who are familiar with the classroom situation and are intimately
and knowledgeably in contact with children, the artist can provide the most legitimate and imaginative leadership in building
an arts curriculum. Educators may be aware of the history of
curriculum development in the arts, which until recently demonstrated this development to be the responsibility of people who
were only tenuously and indirectly related to the arts, or not at
all. The resulting deductive nature of the curriculum development
attempts frequently obscured, distorted, or even falsified the art
experience within educational contexts. At the very least, a secondary and contrived learning climate was instituted, while there
was often a confusion of ends and means. Some change was
needed leading to the artist as primary curriculum builder; having
the artist working in collaborative effort with teachers would be
most salutary and productive. A similar team was projected for
the future with the art critic or aesthetician working with artists
and teachers in order to establish a valid conceptual base for
literacy in the arts. Other specialists would be part of the con-
stellation of curriculum personnel: educators in each of the art
areas, psychologists, childhood education specialists, general curriculum theorists, and educational researchers. However, initial
committee conceptualization was abjured in the belief that the
intactness and validity of the design required the individual creative efforts of the artist-conceptualizer. Once the artist had pre-

sented parts of his curriculum design, it was then subjected to the scrutiny of the other team members. At that point, it could be changed, refined, or even rejected. There were some difficulties in this mix which I will elaborate later.

In discussing the structure of the CAREL process model curriculum we go beyond the initial rationale and on into the actual construction and research implementation of the arts curriculum. The sense of a process model curriculum and the characteristic manner of its development are already manifest in my preceding remarks concerning the theoretical openness of the teaching act and in the ongoing interaction between curriculum makers and their teacher collaborators. A process model curriculum in the arts may be said to function as an open-ended and self-renewing structure establishing a range of concepts, references, and learning experiences which are to be regarded as cues for entering into creative or critical activities in the arts. The model is composed of four parts which are related to one another as the need arises: (1) a conceptual framework; (2) suggested learning experiences for children; (3) guidelines for teachers; and (4) evaluation procedures.

The conceptual framework is not a definitive theory of art in any one of the five areas under consideration. If Plato and Schopenhauer disagree with Dewey or Sartre as to the nature of art, and aestheticians better one another in a confusing medley of analysis, no group of curriculum makers is going to resolve the issues. However, it is possible to identify and liberally organize a set of seminal concepts derived from the working habits and insights of practicing artists concerning the functioning of the arts which may also include various aspects of several art theories or aesthetic attitudes. Their value as they have been developed in the CAREL program lies in providing for teachers an artists' viewpoint which indicates some of the basic and contemporary attributes and processes of a particular art form. Beyond this, but within a context of personal uniqueness and creative immediacy, it is appropriate to entertain the notion that there are certain critical constants, cognitive considerations, and presentational skills which provide a backbone, so to speak, for curriculum research and development in the arts. Each art form establishes a lexicon of concepts which is unique to its expressive and sensory dimensions and particularly characteristic of its creative processes.

These in turn offer a teaching vocabulary and the means for making discriminating choices and relevant relationships which a teacher can order as individual learning occasions require.

For instance, in the visual arts, as in the other arts, two fundamental divisions may be categorized: (1) visual literacy, developing a personal recreation or responsiveness to the world of art and a critical reflection upon its aesthetic qualities, and (2) the making of forms involving a direct participation in studio activities and individual expressiveness. The latter activity utilizes the visual elements (line, color, etc.) to order sensory metaphors which transform the artists' experiences into form. The concepts which may be formulated within one or the other visual category are drawn from observable yet intuitive sensory and perceptual properties from the more cognitive characteristics of critical intelligence or combining the two. These can then take on qualities of expressiveness and artistic significance as they are individually composed into aesthetic relationships.

Briefly, in each of the other four art components, a major concept serves to identify its characteristic quality: in drama, the major concepts are conceived out of mimesis and improvisation; in dance, the concepts consist of space-time-force in dynamic relationship; in literature, the concepts grow out of the imaginative construction of verbal metaphors which unlock the power of language to convey ideas and express feelings; and in music, the inventive use of pitch, timbre, dynamics, rhythm, and form establishes a language of sound with which to express states of being. The concepts present a coherent, if necessarily incomplete framework, and provide, for the teacher, a conjunctively organized but also intuitively felt array of information, or better, insights. The curriculum organization research of Elliot Eisner of Stanford University has been helpful in this area for the visual arts. The description of the interrelatedness of artistic phenomena also offers an inviting base for organizing speculative and expressive ideas and feelings not sequentially but around focal points. Certainly, the thinking of such figures as Susanne Langer, Levi-Strauss, Gombrick, and Arnheim offers pertinent sources for such curricular organization in the arts. The framework thus provides an intellectual structure which relates theory and practice in discernible yet aesthetic ways for teachers and students. The concepts within the framework are laden with enough informative substance to plant the teacher on firm pedagogical ground so she may trust her own approaches, but they are sufficiently nonprescriptive to encourage discovery methods in teaching as well as in learning. Allowance is made for improvisational extensions, for unanticipated and unique attitudes and solutions, all inherent aspects of artistic processes.

The conceptual framework for any one of the art forms is divided into units or lessons, that is, into appropriate designations of materials which most naturally lend themselves to structural discreteness. These become the lesson or set of lessons which a teacher can accept as unitary segments of teaching or learning content. The suggested learning experiences that appear in the curriculum are direct outgrowths of an openly conceived developmental process, the result of the collaborative effort between artist and teacher, each acting as a cross reference or as a "reality check" against the other.

At this point the active developmental nature of the CAREL curriculum spurts into the open; there is loose formative evaluation. The curriculum builder begins to pay a great deal of attention to what actually happens to the substance of his curriculum once it leaves the hallowed precincts of research centers as written documents with or without audio-visual materials. CAREL organized a regular series of continuing workshops in which the mix of curriculum building participants confronted one another's ideas and practices. In the developmental phase, the workshops functioned as centers for substance and process analysis. The teachers could make intense and searching responses to suggested learning experiences in the classroom as well as the workshop and offer their own improvised teaching possibilities for critical review. The resulting dialectic clarified and sharpened the material a curriculum builder inserts in the curriculum. It was based not only on the discussions held between the artists and teachers in an initial phase of conceptualization, but also on an examination of the results of teacher trials of materials. It was explored further as CAREL staff members visited teachers in the classroom during the actual progress of a lesson. There was also an examination of the work produced by the children and staff interactions with them in schools. The work was regarded as part of the total learning process as was the students' verbal and gestural responses, tangible expressions of personal involvement and indicators of artistic growth.

The suggested learning experiences that do become a part of the art curriculum are thus the result of an active process with a number of clarifying stages. However, even the revised curriculum offered to all teachers was not a codified package. At the very least, varying alternatives to eliciting appropriate classroom experiences were listed so that teachers could examine the values of feasibility and choice in art. In some instances, there were no actual suggested experiences but rather an evocative presentation of qualities characterizing a particular concept.

The need for subsequent teacher in-service workshops rests on the supposition that abstractly conceived and written materials are insufficient guides for the teacher inexperienced in the arts or, for that matter, often for the experienced teacher as well. Teachers need to be trained in depth in the use of curriculum materials, especially those which demand aesthetic and qualitative understanding. The CAREL program envisioned continuous teacher workshops as a necessary corollary to any written material in order to effect the most desirable implementation of a genuine arts philosophy in the schools. This was in response to what was perhaps the most pervasive problem encountered in the development of arts curricula, reaching the teachers in such a way as to evoke their own sensitivity and personal absorption in the arts. The characteristic training of elementary school teachers leaves much to be desired in the development of creative and aesthetic sensibility, while their involvement with culture tends toward homogeneous attitudes.

Thus, flexibility and open alternative organization in the arts are stressed in a process model curriculum. This may be disturbing, but it is challenging to teachers. The substance of the curriculum is specifically relevant on its conceptual level, but is regarded as subject to continuing identification and interpretation on its implementing level, stressing teacher involvement and particularized translation in the classroom. This approach is further elaborated in the guidelines provided for teachers. The guidelines offer speculations on methods, explanations of hypotheses, examinations of objectives, a listing of necessary teacher preparations, sources for materials, and some in-depth discussion of the art content. In short, they provide a succinct exposition of the background information which could be useful to teachers in structuring their lessons and in conveying the sense of the lesson focus. Attempts are made to write guides imaginatively, not only to enliven the content but to ensure that teachers will read them.

The area of evaluation has been a difficult and thorny one for the CAREL program. There is no basic or common evaluative framework which can unequivocally measure or judge the inherently creative, critical, and affective dimensions of artistic and aesthetic experience. Indeed, it is also questionable if ways can be devised or instruments constructed which would pursue such evaluation goals. Yet, somehow curriculum builders and teachers alike need to know whether they do in fact achieve what they set out to do. It is a legitimate question to ask in the abstract, but a slippery one to pin down in artistic and aesthetic matters, even in educational contexts. The danger in the arts area, as in most other disciplines, lies in the narrow structuring of curricula which can be measured, in teaching only that which can be explicitly evaluated, and in equating curriculum research and development with evaluation. Even a hint of such an approach to curriculum making in the arts negates the very qualities of imaginative expressiveness and unique resolution which enrich the art experience and give it its most characteristic image.

The CAREL program began to resolve some of its evaluation problems by indicating the need to depart markedly from the criteria utilized for quantitative methodologies of evaluative analysis. A major commitment in evaluation became that of inquiring into the very nature of what constitutes evaluation in the arts and what should be the significant outcomes in arts education. Another proposed functional description of evaluation derived from the internal components of the process model itself. Such an approach would formulate goals, experimental development, and behavioral changes as they relate to the conceptual framework. The actual participation in various creatively artistic and responsive activities would serve as "operational" levels, with the teacher or observer making critical judgments based on an aesthetic mode of inquiry to be developed in the curriculum. These considerations are qualitative rather than quantitative. They are expressed, for example, in the use of color, in the vividness of metaphoric imagery, in the dynamic delineation of space, in the utilization of rhythmic patterns, but especially in the way in which an individual sets these elements into relationship. The keenness of observation, the ability to relate interpretive insights to formal qualities, and other critical abilities would also serve as evaluation counters. All of the foregoing need to be related to the individual student who should be evaluated in terms of his own capacities, level of maturation, value structure, and organization of skills. The basis for some means of pertinent "measurement" lies in the child's participation in the artistic and critical processes. The latter then establishes an interrelationship between the problems which are implicitly as well as explicitly formulated in the curriculum and those which a child poses for himself or derives directly from a lesson. The interrelationship may be evaluated, but so must the child's own statement of an artistic problem and its resolution. Conceivably, the process remains open-ended in that specific artistic resolutions and behavioral goals are experimentally and functionally developed rather than beholden to predetermined ends. Criteria are present, but as creative agents in a creative process rather than as immutable landmarks which must be acknowledged on the way to anticipated goals.

It may be possible to apply a similar process to the teacher's progress toward the attainment of goals in the teaching of art, and CAREL made some attempts in that direction. However, it also utilized more traditional questionnaires and journal keeping methods as well as trained observer evaluations. Overall, the area of evaluation in arts curriculum development remains a rather uncertain one, requiring further exploration and, for a while perhaps, a "mad money" economics of support.

It should be understood that the process model arts curricula are not directories of parts or manuals of instruction. They are not designed in any "how-to-do-it" fashion or as sequentially organized or graded series of lessons requiring group mimesis or rote adherence. Rather, the curricula are only stimulating, suggestive, and advisory guides opening on to creative process in art and in education, establishing viable yet genuinely artistic criteria. The curricula are thus experientially oriented, respecting contingency and individuality over a linear profession of predetermined skills and sequential activities.

However, there were many problems to be overcome before the

CAREL program arrived at the relatively cohesive position which has been outlined. As the program moved into creating its position, it continued to suffer from the difficulties of its initial conceptualization, but not nearly as much as from the confused cross-purposes that arose during its first year of development. Conceivably, these cross-purposes led to the demise of the laboratory. Certainly, under the auspices of a government funding institution there could be no such creative bumbling or productive contentiousness as occurred at CAREL. The evaluative guidelines too narrowly defined clarity of purpose and efficiency of procedure. The ambiguities of the arts in education cannot find their way in the narrow confines which the quota procedure of ideas imposes. They may need more theoretical and developmental elbow room than some other research areas. In any case, a basic problem in developing fresh and speculative curriculum conceptualization has been "how to stay in business." Certainly, it would seem that a "mad money" approach in the arts area may pay off simply by removing unnecessary pressures which defeat many of the goals of curriculum building in the arts.

However, I can point to abrasive and difficult problems which the CAREL arts curriculum development has had to face and somehow resolve. A primary one has been the selection of personnel to carry on research and development in the arts. This is of course intimately tied to the alternative choices to be made. Which philosophical or conceptual systems would most logically and expressively convey or express the sense of the arts and the objectives it sets for its role in education? Which methods of examination and development and which theoretical, if any, guidelines can best structure curricula in the arts? This has been a devastatingly complex issue which, perhaps, questions the very raison d'être behind all curriculum development. Another large problem area has been that of the political dimensions of prevailing educational influences compounded by the careerism of individuals on the lower as well as the higher rungs of institutional ladders. And finally there are the cultural forces and influences which impinge upon what a curriculum developer does and how he does it. In most ways these problem areas are very much related, producing cross-fertilization of frustration as well as finally ending up as "one big headache." However, facetiousness aside, the problems are vital reflections of some of the more dynamic aspects of the contemporary scene and as such are welcome goals which set creative tensions for creative spirits.

Responsible as well as creative spirits, curriculum makers are obligated to view the culture they live in with a critical and discerning eye. For instance, schools like to believe that they are the principal agent of education in the country. In a formal academic way this may still be so especially if one accepts nicely delineated disciplines as the transmittal contexts for education. However, it would be difficult to disprove an even greater educational impact upon Americans exerted by the mass media and popular culture. True, such influences are somewhat informal and diverse. They are also persistent, ubiquitous, rather fundamental, and frequently unconscious. Thus, electronic media, advertising, the camera image, and all of the other attendant communications paraphernalia of popular culture tend to displace the intellectual, graded and curricular structuring of the classroom. Vivid graphics, television, the film, and mixed audio and visual media act as vigorous and multi-dimensioned agents of education. Because these areas of information and insight which extend peremptorily to the classroom are so prevalent and insinuating, the informal education can take on aspects of conditioning and manipulation.

The outside influences are felt in the classroom via the media manipulated student and his conditioned sensibility. Teachers, who are often the epitome of middle-class values to which mass media is largely directed, are also the target of graphic communications. Their personalities as well as the patterns of their teaching reflect a public consciousness. Though such patterns are not to be faulted, per se, it is possible to question their impact upon aspirations toward educational excellence. They may demonstrate a lack of awareness to the private and expressive needs of individuals which the conditioning of mass media and popular culture characteristically generates.

Education in the arts finds itself just as much subject to the blandishments and forms of mass communications as any other educational area. Perhaps, it is even more influenced in the case of art education in that it shares the physical and artistic properties of the pervading popular culture. Certainly many of the art education practices in the classroom possess more than a passing relationship to the outside commercial and communications environment. The philosophic base of education in the arts has also been intruded upon by a sense of the inordinate press of public culture. There is currently among theorists a rather broad re-examination of earlier premises and future objectives, not the least of which is forced by the activity of popular culture as it impinges upon the classroom.

As a consequence, the curriculum makers need to consider seriously the relationship of arts education to mass media and popular culture. At least they need to pose some relevant issues, to raise pertinent questions, and to offer beginning educational resolutions or guidelines for action. The latter would be hopefully open-ended recommendations which would alert administrators, teachers, and students to the changing forces of their environment and the dynamic but value laden interrelationships that are shaping the energies of both individual personalities and cultural patterns.

I would like to speculate more in depth upon at least one of the problems the CAREL program encountered and some resolutions offered, though I am certain there will be more questions implied than resolutions described. The problem grows out of the assumption in high places that the social sciences, most particularly those with quantifiable behavioral parameters, can produce foolproof indicators of appropriateness and excellence in almost any discipline. Characteristically, the educational establishment set about its task of initial planning for CAREL in a ritually institutional manner. It created, through its blandly arrogant imposition of methodology, not only creatively posed problems but also obstructive ones which have plagued the arts curriculum program for much of its duration. The most disastrous problem has been an indiscriminate initial acceptance of behavioral objectives as the prism through which curriculum development in the arts was to be conceived. This approach, though it aimed at innovation, grew out of current orthodoxy. In retrospect it may be seen as the result of political influences in education and fashionable research mores as much as a rationally conceived approach to arts education. The planners also erred at this stage in failing to consult with any appropriate people in the arts, deepening the initial proceedings as an in-house affair.

In any case, an extended conference was convened in the summer of 1967 to develop the behavioral structure in the arts for curriculum building purposes. Teams were made up in each of the five areas composed of a practicing artist, or, in some instances, an active educator in the arts, and classroom teachers. Consulting personnel were also available: psychologists, early childhood specialists, educational administrators and coordinators, as well as a variety of others. Over a six-week period the teams in each of the art areas were to designate goals or objectives in a definitive manner and to operationalize the nature of the art form in behavioral terms. Theoretically the blend of the arts specialist and teacher attuned to classroom conditions conceptualizing in tandem and in egalitarian delight would produce a sound basis for curriculum development in the arts, aided and abetted by hovering psychologists and high-powered theoretical educators. To this end the participants were instructed quite intensively in Mager's behavioral dictums. I will not go into the painful recital of what occurred — or perhaps I should say in developmental terms what did not occur. Some antagonized group dynamics resulted in an abortive accumulation of irrelevant data which, it was doggedly insisted, should be utilized willy-nilly during the ensuing year. It took a good deal of vociferous destruction to offset what can only be referred to as the pernicious influence of strict behavioral objectives in an arts curriculum development.

I shall point up only a few of the anomalies, contradictions, and disturbing elements which existed on a practical as well as a theoretical level. For one, it was quite wasteful to put together during the initial phases arbitrarily chosen and artistically commonplace teachers with highly sophisticated artists for a specified period of time. One group could not honestly communicate with the other — the spread was simply too great. Then, too, though the artists were chosen with some discernment, the teachers were selected on the basis of irrelevant geographical and racial factors. Actually, what was needed were highly intelligent, experienced, and enthusiastic teachers who could enter into the dynamics of the interchange with more than pious hopes. The pattern of development was doomed, in any case. The behavioral-objective syndrome simply could not encompass the most fundamental aspects of the role and function of the arts in education in other than an atomistically fragmented and externally simplistic manner.

Without any real in-depth analysis, permit me to list the major limitations of behavioral objectives in developing curriculum, at least in the arts. It creates among curriculum developers the illusion that it can solve the major problems of conceptualization and structuring when in fact in concentrating upon narrowly extrinsic manifestations of behavioral change, it is only looking at the iceberg above the water level, ignoring its vast hidden, yet controlling structure. Another limitation is its standardization of artistic elements and processes although the elements and processes are, in fact, quite unique and open-ended as they are creatively utilized by artists and students. Also limiting is the advance specification of particular creative experiences as predetermined objectives, despite the very flexible and rather unanticipated resolutions to problems which the artistic process does generate. At the very least, the behavioral objectives lead teachers to believe that the specified outcomes are the really significant and acceptable ones. The stress upon measurement and evaluation also structures the curriculum, as mentioned earlier, so that only those activities which are amenable to measurement are included. Most important, the methodology of behavioral objectives misses the broadly ambiguous and metaphoric spirit of the arts and tends to put obstacles in the way of both refined individual teaching styles and imaginative improvisational or fresh resolutions to artistic problems.

However, the experience of attempting to deal with behavioral objectives was a salubrious and productive one in some respects, particularly as it sharpened the reactions that were elicited, leading to more appropriate theorizing and relevant organization. Some comment upon related but more generalized influences in curriculum building which create problems of method and goal definition in the arts may be worthwhile at this point.

More often than not the rationale presented in developmental arts curriculum programs is couched in solemn, over-elaborate and even contradictory terms. It pays pious lip service to the creatively fertilizing and aesthetically satisfying aspects of art. Yet, because of cultural constraints, professional orthodoxy, and a philosophical allegiance to a so-called clarity and efficiency, it insists upon bending the functions and forms of art of particular ends and procedures and it ends up processing individuals as well as predetermining method. This reinforces a sentimentalized, superficial, and standardized understanding of the role of art and its functions, not only in education, but in life as well, breeding a mediocrity, if not a philistinism, of the spirit and the senses.

In truth, the antic and amorphous stimulation arising out of inner urging should animate curriculum building in the arts and sometimes does so, if unwittingly. Some common core of collective delight and personal realization makes itself felt, even if on an unconscious level. The arts are naturally sensed as necessary aspects of living education: their attributes of play, expressiveness, and intrinsically significant meaning, their vivid sensations which open up into surprise-laden perceptions, their intriguing ambiguities and intuitive resolutions which intensify feeling and sentience, their private intimacy even during public exposure, their sheer and utter uselessness which generates innate and priceless satisfactions, their civilizing passions and symbolic potentialities are all apprehended in one way or another. Curriculum research in the arts needs to be touched by the latter generous and experientially unfolding humanism as well as by the search for understanding the more rationally and abstractly ordered elements of cognition, judgment, and skills procedures. "It needs to reinstate the vague and inarticulate to its proper place in our mental life" as William James advocated. Therein lies the "art" of curriculum building in the arts, but it is not deliberately attended to nor respected in many instances. This neglect results in the restrictive solemnity and self-defeating contradictions which constipate or distort many curriculum-building attempts in the arts. It is necessary that the shapers of curriculum permit, rather encourage, a confrontation between sentience and experience in ways other than those of systematic or quantitative definition.

Many of the faulty and unfitting directions apparent in the development of arts curriculum over the past decade or two need to be seen also within the larger context of the curriculum reform movement. As an aside, though, it may be candidly stated that most theorists in arts education rarely consulted content professionals or area scholars, in contrast to curriculum builders in the natural and physical sciences. Instead, they relied heavily on the behavioral and social sciences, treating their own content and area practitioners as if they were happenstance and only of minor importance if not actually harmful.

The unseemly orientation toward the hard precision of science offset the softer ambiguous but nonetheless legitimate approaches of aesthetic and artistic modes. By structuring subject disciplines and directing research in this manner, confusion and contradiction are compounded in setting up developmental guidelines. Most obvious has been the acceptance of conceptual models which merged substance, procedures, and performance into highly rational and objective patterns, generally within the strict behavioral considerations that have been mentioned. This was the coherent and unified approach many researchers had felt was needed. Such objectified models, controlled with relative ease and lending themselves to simplified implementation established seemingly functional criteria for evaluative purposes. Governmental and institutional administrators could then rely upon investigators who would plan, or at least attempt to plan the entire process of curriculum research and consequent reform, like the cartographer diagramming his maps before he explores the terrain or an auditor ticking off different parts of a ledger. The educational researcher was in a position to tell you where he had been, who was there with him and what route they took, even if the trip was an imaginary one. In terms of public accountability he could give evidence of evaluation: he could count noses, offer statistical relationships leading to cause-and-effect equations, and finally provide a kind of educational cost-accounting, a quantitative measure. These enumerations may all be basic to areas of civic responsibility if not political orthodoxy, but they are questionable educationally and also existentially. The Establishment in education, which had read the handwriting on the wall of curriculum reform rather later than it should have, could thereby recoup its position of leadership, a position under consistent attack by the critics of education.

As substance was reduced to its supposed operational structure, a myth of methodology came into being which permitted the ready processing of content, learning patterns, and teaching dynamics. Clarity, precision, and logical explicitness or sequence became not only methodological guideposts but rigorous measures of adequacy in both research and implementation. Cognitive delineation took hold. Though there was a realization that emotions, imagination, and intuition are inherent elements in human growth and education, they were accepted only on a specified operational level rather than on a broadly experiential one. There could be no acceptance of Louis Armstrong's answer to the question: What is Jazz? "If I have to explain it, you'll never understand."

In short, curriculum reform assumed a technical stance. The dialectics of curriculum building were wound tight. There was a

general abjuration of procedural ambiguity, of what was considered to be the slovenly structure of intuitive insights or the un-
amenably vague or vacillating parameters of imagination or
feeling. The latter, typically bound up with values and idiosyncratic attributes, simply were not to be quantified or objectively
evaluated. They could not be logically formulated in explicit or
very discrete ways, nor would they fit into any neat, sequentially
calibrated schemata. Consequently those qualities of experience
or learning which were discontinuous and private, largely subjective, and dependent on flashes of intuition or of emotional and
particularly imaginative composing were largely ignored or rejected. Those worlds of feeling and understanding which provide
elegance, beauty, and expressiveness — the other than observably
pragmatic meanings of life — were effectively sloughed off, even
in those disciplines which are centrally characterized by such
values and qualities, as are the arts. If experience could not be
reduced to words, and precise ones as that, or could not be plotted
on quantifiable grids, it simply was not to be heeded.

I am unable to develop an analysis of such conditions from
the vantage point of the professional philosopher nor does space
permit any extended examination of the underlying forces which
reflect the varying views concerning who and what is man, views
which forcefully influence the construction of curriculum and the
nature of learning in all areas. Perhaps, I can sum it up by saying
that we need to sense the motivating distinctions between two very
current life styles — that of the technician against that of the
hippie, or if that is too far out, that of the artist. In the ensuing
dialectics and dialogue there may be some helpful understandings
as to which life style offers the most appropriate guidelines. We
may find that it is necessary to create a third image, combining
the best of the other two in order to make the most vital yet reasonable resolution to the problems of curriculum construction.
However, such a merging may process elements of wishful thinking; the antagonists may be mutually exclusive.

There appears, nevertheless, to be philosophical and professional danger in seriously suggesting that there are artistic elements and cultural influences which may be utilized theoretically
in structuring a curriculum or pragmatically in shaping its implementation. Against the prevailing behavioral orthodoxy and

reverent respect for scientific-like methodology, such notions can be regarded as sheer heresy or addleheaded nonsense. Of course such attitudes are reinforced when one can observe the erratic intrigues of culture and the ambiguous functions of art. Yet art and culture survive, and the modes of inquiry and insight peculiar to art at least continue to create new truths. It is with such belief that I can declare any curriculum to be no more than a multidimensional metaphor, made up of viable possibilities and suggestive cues.

The distinctive value of the arts and humanities in education is in the continuing realization of the self. If such a value is accepted, any approach to education, or any innovative intent, must allow for the characteristically affective and intuitive modes of interaction with experience, along with the cognitive. Attitudes and values, those soft areas which inform and enrich perception, understanding, and knowledge, are also integral aspects of the processes that refine and expand human sentience and actions. The arts, to which these qualitites are idiomatic, intensify those human sensibilities and creative capacities of a nondiscursive nature, making of man more than a mere thinking reed. The consequent expressive autonomy establishes an experiential base for creative learning. Some sense of these qualitative processes and aesthetic attributes needs to be built into the tenor of curriculum guidelines, into the very methodologies employed to achieve organization and implementation.

Such attitudes embodied in the construction of curriculum would naturally abet the development of a hospitable climate within which the humanistic educational aims of a realization of the self and a heightened awareness of the world can be achieved. For students and teachers alike, the experience is outside the pale of strictly rational or pragmatic concerns. The necessarily varying and alternative attempts at curriculum building in the arts are thus fulfilling volatile though profound human aspirations frequently below the threshold of consciousness, but as old and continuing as the hills. The actual denouement, whether as crystallized conceptualization or as classroom experience, is necessarily vital and dynamic and also often tentative. It accepts existential contingency as a base of relationship much as the hills waken each morning to sunshine or rain, cold or heat, and forag-

ing hunters or tender lovers. Any curriculum building, at least in
the arts, needs to recognize the unfixed nature of the efforts that
shape its form.

Curriculum building in the arts of a germane nature is a consistently open yet rigorous affair and is characteristically unfinished yet encompassing in its development. Paradoxically, as a
curriculum program in the arts establishes a lexicon of content
and method, it is subjected to the transiency of its singularly
shifting context and the uniquely variable qualities of personal
experience. The process is a reminder of T. S. Eliot's lines:
"every attempt is a wholly new start, and a different kind of
failure." However, such "failure" may be creatively exciting and
educationally rewarding. Each can permit and encourage within
an aesthetic ambience, a qualitative intelligence and a sensitized
subjectivity with which to encounter the stuff of living in vivid
and fresh ways. Any arts curriculum construction needs to aim
at enhancing both sensation and sentience in the classroom. Yet
a felt and intelligent involvement with these human attributes
that lead to perception and understanding demand that educational guides, like the very nature of art, respect individual differences, subjective responses, and varying life styles. They should
assist teachers and students to shape their experiences in their
individual, yet critically qualitative ways. Curriculum in the arts
functions most effectively as it offers alternatives rather than
prescriptions, counsel rather than exhortation, suggestive cues
rather than directives, points from which to begin rather than
points at which to end.

Edmund Burke Feldman

Comments on

THE ART OF CURRICULUM
MAKING IN THE ARTS

I expect that you were overwhelmed, as I was, by Kaufman's
address. One of the consequences of being overwhelmed is the
difficulty of dealing very adequately with so massive a report on

a curriculum development project covering all the arts. I shall attempt what might be called a free translation.

I think the first impression that emerges from the document — and there is no way to get around it — is that this particular curriculum project was a failure. This impression is gained from the fact that the project was terminated by the CAREL Educational Laboratory and that the author reports some unhappy times experienced by the curriculum consultants and the project administrators. Kaufman devotes considerable space to describing how people were assembled, how they tried to reach their decisions, how they set up their guiding assumptions, etc. A great deal of time was spent on "tooling up," but relatively little curriculum material was produced. I suppose that part of the failure has to be attributed to some of these procedures. Some of the words and phrases that are characteristic of the report reflect a tendency to substitute noble educational language for the hard job of curriculum decision-making. We have expressions like "sensitive responses," "creative learning," "vivid way of learning," "personal validity," "there is no right answer in art, there is only the right answer for the child," "inherently sufficient activity," "instrinsic experience," etc. In addition, I detected traces of an attitude toward art teaching that I call the Metro-Goldwyn-Mayer philosophy of art. You remember the lion that comes on the screen and roars, while underneath appears a Latin phrase which can be translated as "art for the sake of art." If Sam Goldwyn meant art for the sake of money he would have been more truthful. But Kaufman truly believes art is its own excuse for being, even in a school context. If kids cannot create authentic art, they must at least be taught by authentic artists. As a teacher, the author brings to the art of curriculum building the experience of a painter who has exhibited regularly and who obviously has considerable faith in the educational insights of the producing artist. He feels the artist has a more authentic grasp of the factors entering into the creative situation than anyone else. To be sure, an artist has to feel this way in today's frantic art scene; otherwise he might give up his creative search. It is precisely this confidence — so vital for the professional survival of the artist — that manifests itself as a certain lack of tolerance for the contributions of the other people who work in the area of curriculum construction, and who have, conceivably, some wisdom to bring to the process. We have all suffered in our education from the instruction of teachers who do not seem to have had any authentic experience with the artistic or scientific disciplines they teach about. Still, we have also learned that some critics, historians, and educators do have valid insights into the character of the arts. It seems to me there are several sources of wisdom for curriculum building in the arts and humanities. But apparently Kaufman has laid it down as a principle, almost theologically, that the committed artist alone has insight into art. Anything others say or do has to conform to the artist's understanding about what learning in art is and what artistic creativity is. When we initiate curriculum building experience with this rather exclusionary policy, we surely antagonize the people whose help we shall need along the way. I mention this point as a comment on administrative strategy.

There is also implicit in the discussion a notion that art education embraces essentially the business of making art. And the making of art today is understood largely in terms of the artistic situation since the end of the French and American Revolutions. That is, the artist creates art independently and hopes someone will buy what he has made. I need not tell you that art has been created since man has been man and that many kinds of relations have existed between artists and patrons. The most recent model of that relationship may not be the best one for education.

The history of art embraces the history of artistic creativity under virtually all conditions of man, under all forms of social organization, in all areas of the earth. When we base our thinking about teaching in this area on what is visible in the Metropolitan Museum or at the Chicago Art Institute or in the galleries on 57th Street, we are indeed looking at the top of the iceberg. When we have an image of the artist based on his life in a garrett, based on *La Vie bohème* perhaps, or today's careerist seeking foundation support or a gallery connection, I submit we have a distorted image of who the artist is, what art is, and consequently what art education can be. Instead, we have today a wonderful opportunity in education to build curricula upon a comprehensive idea of art based on all periods of artistic creativity rather than the recent, limited, and possibly atypical experience of man with art.

There was a failure of communication, Kaufman tells us, within the curriculum team he had assembled representing the several arts specializations. I think others have had a similar experience. The separate languages of the arts, despite what Virgil said many years ago ("All the arts are interrelated"), tend to divide us. And while some of us have hope of a team approach to art instruction in the schools, I have come to the view that the aesthetic education of children can best be accomplished through in-depth instruction in one of the arts, any one of them. It is not necessary for every young-ster to be a Renaissance man — to be at once a musician, a poet, an essayist, a visual arts performer, an athlete, and a scientist too. But in the public schools we seem to assume that the production of the *uomo universale* is the goal of the curriculum. I would be very content, of course, if we could do a good job of general education through the visual arts. I hope that our colleagues in music and literature will seek the same goal through their disciplines. But let us keep in mind the dual character of art education — artistic performance and what is called art *appreciation*. The latter is a poor term. It means understanding art, criticizing art, judging art. Kaufman appears to be hung up on the difficulty of con-ceptualizing or verbalizing subjective states. Hence his emphasis is on artistic performance. Obviously he feels that this is the essence of the art program and that appreciative and critical modes of learning are beyond teaching. But I don't think this is the central problem with respect to aesthetic education. Also, I don't think the existence of curricula in the arts has to result in freezing out unanticipated learning by students. I think we can design curricula — we *have* designed curricula — which permit all kinds of improvised learning and discovery among students in the characteristic realms of the arts. There are many teachers who can walk into a classroom and dream up superlative teaching practices as they go through the door. A teacher need not feel constrained by the fact that he works within a curriculum. In other words, we may be confronted with a false dilemma in the implied notion that planning and evaluating the art program re-sults in the sacrifice of its vital juices. This whole business of subjective responses being recalcitrant to observation and mea-surement can be erected into a device for avoiding any systematic scrutiny of our teaching. But I think that the problem is im-properly stated. There are all kinds of ways to find out how people feel and think in the presence of work of art. We are not so naive as to think verbal responses are identical to aesthetic feelings. Still, we can submit verbal responses to some kind of measurement and quantification without having any illusions about the precision of these measurements. The results are sufficient to guide instruction and to correct curriculum strategies; that is mainly what we are interested in.

We also know a great deal about the subject matter of art. I mean that the history of art, art criticism, and aesthetics have accumulated a tremendous amount of data. There are many styles of study in art history and they are all available to us if we want to use them. I will mention only one distinguished artist historian, Heinrich Wölfflin, who wrote the *Principles of Art History*. He established the modern foundations for examining art styles and even developed what he believed to be the laws of changing visual perception in human societies. We haven't begun to exploit this material in curriculum development — for example, in teaching the development from linear forms to painterly forms, the evolution from closed form to open form, from clarity to indistinctness, from planar space to recessional space. These categories for describing and analyzing works of art are available to us in teaching if we would use them.

The history of art ranges very widely over time and space. To be sure, the scholarship about it has been rather ethnocentric; it is often excessively nationalistic; it is open to criticism because it has ignored the art of what we used to call savages — the art of the people in the Third World. It needs to be rewritten. Nevertheless, there is a tremendous amount of valuable material there to build on. There is also a large body of art criticism; it comes to us in verbal form and it constitutes an objectification of subjective and aesthetic responses. Art criticism furnishes the curriculum maker with a range of material that is substantially parallel to what is available to teachers of literature. We also know a great deal about artistic development in childhood and adolescence as it is related to the psychological stages of development. This is fairly hard data, and it constitutes a body of information on which teaching practices and curriculum sequences can be developed. In addition, there is a considerable literature on perceptual theory with which most learning psychologists are familiar.

A neglected source of information for art education is anthropology. I sometimes feel anthropologists are a more fertile source of information than art historians because they take the complete human condition as their province rather than the history of art that is visible in galleries and museums. The whole man-made world is grist for our mill. The entire designed environment, everything that is shaped and formed by man, becomes the subject matter of aesthetic education. All of these visual and conceptual materials, of course, have to enter the experience of pupils — poor and rich, black and white, young and old. They comprise the stuff of which curricula and teaching practices can be fashioned.

Let me discuss in general terms a theory of aesthetic education. I believe it ought to embrace four categories. These should designate the kinds of learning that are possible as a result of reasonably serious encounters with the arts, any of the arts. The first kind is cognitive learning. This type of learning embraces more than the titles and the names of artists, the dates of their work, and the usual rather dull memorization of style sequences. I am talking about what is learned when we show works of art to kids who are building a primary vocabulary of words and perceptual images for dealing with objects, ideas, and concepts. There is nothing terribly mysterious about cognitive study through art. When you show a work of art to kids they want to talk about it, to tell you what they see; they want to name and describe things. A fairly unsophisticated strategy of questioning elicits inferences about the qualities of the things they have named. The work of art — any work of art — is a system of signs and symbols having some relation to the world. And we can begin the work of developing visual literacy by learning how to read or interpret those signs and symbols and their relationship to the world. The child does not encounter reality directly through art; he encounters it at one or two steps removed. He must learn, like all of us, to deal with reality through a language — in our case, a visual language.

A second type of learning occurs through what I call linguistic study — learning the language of art the way one learns a foreign language, that is, learning the grammar and syntax of art. I call it learning the styles of art, the several modes of visual expression. It is tremendously important to learn how to read style. I think kids have to read style in school in order to survive outside of school. They have to learn to read the styles of television and magazine presentations and they have to perceive juxatapositions of electronic and printed imagery as vehicles of meaning. You may say this constitutes using art instrumentally, the equivalent of maintaining that art is not as important as something else. But in an educational context we *have* to use art instrumentally. As far as I am concerned, art is not an end in itself. That is a nine-teenth-century obsession and I think we have long suffered from it in art education. We are still influenced by the kind of educa-tion that was enjoyed by aristocratic English gentlemen who spent a year abroad after completing several years of sherry drinking at Oxford or Cambridge. They had to learn the names of Greek, Roman, and Italian monuments of art in order to report them back to friends and relatives after the *Wanderjahr* was over. My point is that the class education of the past seems to become the popular education of the present so far as the arts are concerned.

A third kind of learning I call intermedia study. In order to cope with the world, you have to be able to translate from one language to another — from or to a visual language, a kinetic language, an aural language, an oral language. You have to be able to translate what you see into what you say and do. Today, we have to move between media fluently. I am perhaps using McLuhan's notion of a medium. I think a moving bus or truck is a type of medium, the kind a kid in the slums often learns to use. He can climb on to a moving bus, figure out its acceleration, and manage to get off it safely. I think that any kid who can manage that sort of task is a smart youngster. He knows how to function within the constraints of a medium, but it is not a medium which is taught in the schools. Alas! The schools do not show him how to translate from his familiar medium into a language of theirs.

The fourth category of aesthetic learning is what I call critical study. By critical study I mean the ability to describe, analyze, interpret, and — in some cases — judge an organized form of visual expression. I am not as much interested in judgment as I am interested in interpretation, because the latter is where the educational payoff is, in my opinion. For one thing, interpretive statements can be examined, they can be analyzed, quantified, and evaluated, whereas critical judgments open up Pandora's box in teaching contexts. Critical interpretation, in my view, is almost identical with teaching. That is, interpreting experiences which happen to be embodied in visual imagery constitutes the main job of the art teacher. Furthermore, we can teach teachers to be critics and we can teach them to base their criticism on their own life experience. It is not necessary for them to accumulate a vast body of prerequisite cognitive material before they can function adequately as critics. We just show them how to systematize their normal habits of drawing inferences from their visual perceptions. It isn't hard.

Let me mention one thing more on the role of critical study in art education. The key problem is how to interpret what you see. You have to translate what you see into language which can be publicly reported to your peers. Some think that you must teach kids a special verbal language with which to encounter art; I don't. I have some doctoral students who are working with black kids who do not have very strong verbal skills. We simply by-pass the problem of whether they know the difference between impressionism and postimpressionism, whether they can use these terms correctly as critics and historians define them. Instead, we let them use their so-called "hip" jargon to talk about what they see and as a result they respond to works of art in a delightful and insightful way. They tell you things about a picture that you never dreamed of, and they do not lie either; they are honestly telling you what they encounter in a work of art. This experience leads us to conclude that we need a supportive atmosphere in the schools to confirm that what they see and report is valid as aesthetic response. We need to establish a model of discourse about art that can serve them as a model for discourse about life.

FIVE

RESPONSIBLE
CURRICULUM DEVELOPMENT

I. INTRODUCTION

I should like to begin my remarks by saying that I believe most curriculum development today to be irresponsible, both in its developmental processes and in the intellectual tools that are used.

Responsibility I take to mean respond-ability in terms of criteria which account adequately for the major variables and kinds of persons rightfully involved in the phenomenological context of schooling. Most current and recent (and not so recent) curriculum developments have not had this respond-ability. Rather than sensitive and emergent happenings of their human contexts, they are more like technical one-dimensional arrows shot into the school situation. As such they have a tendency to rupture the educational process and reduce it to bloody rivulets of memorization, passive conformity, and training exercises.

This lack of responsibility is not intentional. Although one could at times get the impression that some curriculum projects exist and have existed for the benefit of their directors, graduate students, universities and/or development centers, this surely would not be true of many. At least I would prefer to believe, for example, that the entrance of so-called scholars and others into school curriculum development and projects was not primarily due to availability of funds and other advantages, but was mainly motivated by desires for improving the quality of education.

This lack of responsibility lies in the failure of curriculum developers to respond to the total context of our curriculum needs and problems — a sin of omission, caused by ignorance or tunnel vision, rather than one of commission. This failure has extended to many professional educators (who ought to have known better) as well as to most academicians.

Further evidence of poor respond-ability can be seen in the built-in rigidity of developmental processes. By the very nature of present national curriculum project procedures, for example, the possibility of creative response to a complex school milieu is almost impossible.

Having made this major assertion of irresponsibility, I would like to proceed to develop it in detail and conclude with the suggestion of what a responsible model of curriculum development might look like.

Implicit in the position presented here is the assumption that education as an area of study or as a discipline, if you wish, is one of the practical arts. That is, education as a subject belongs in the category of the humanities and not the sciences. Perhaps at one time it would have been called one of the moral sciences, but certainly, like politics, its activity is made up of problems in social policy, social decision-making, and social action. These all demand alternatives, choices, values, and action. Schooling is a process of encountering what society thinks one *ought* to learn, not what there *is* to learn. There is no *objectively discoverable curriculum* to be found "out there."

The implications of this assertion are that the logic of the aesthetic, social, and moral disciplines is more central and appropriate for curriculum development than the logic of scientific or technological areas.

Education deals with cultural forms, one set of which are the sciences and their technologies and languages, but it deals with these forms in the spirit and logic of the humanities. The spirit and/or logic has been called by Ernst Cassirer the logic of "concrete universals" (rather than abstract universals). The mode of inquiry for curriculum is primarily synthesis, not analysis. We are, in other words, dealing with reality not at the basic sense perception level, but at the level of perception of expression (symbolic manifestation). Curriculum development is always evaluative thinking, not objective theoretical thought. Thus, as Levi-

Strauss says about the humanities, we deal with metaphors, not cause-effect chains. In curriculum development we put people together with events and discover what structure of learning emerges; whereas in a scientific enterprise we would start with the structure (theory) and discover the events.

A curriculum ought to be a vehicle for the unfolding of alternatives, with a many-valued focus; not the result of the elimination of alternatives or a single-valued point to be arrived at.

We should be able to put the scientific-technical approach to curriculum development to rest rather easily, if for no other reason than the obvious inability to evaluate the outcomes of schooling in large-scale social terms or long-range personal terms. Experiencing a curriculum should result in what Dewey called the release of capacity, or what Bronowski identifies as self-knowledge. A curriculum is like a *Hamlet,* not like a natural "law." It exists for the individual learners and is justified in terms of these learners, rather than as a thing in its own right. Like *Hamlet* it has both form and structure, a story line, characters, etc., and it reflects disciplined thinking. But what one takes away is not "the" interpretation of *Hamlet,* but an enlargement of personal insight and identifiable alternatives. And it is in this sense that curriculum development should be a process of the creation of the best possible range of alternatives for students.

II. THE PROBLEM OF GOALS AND/OR OBJECTIVES

Although most persons involved in curriculum development will only admit to one, there are at least two basic goals of curricula: (1) the development of the academic mentality and (2) the development of the intellectual mentality. Now, although no one would admit (or perhaps like to think) that school curricula are proposed and developed primarily to produce academics, this accomplishment is, I suggest, the most effective outcome of present-day schooling.

Some academics are intellectuals, of course, but being a well-schooled academic, as evidenced by mastery (mastering the knowledge of a discipline), does not ensure that this knowledge or any other knowledge the academic might possess will be applied intelligently. Knowledge is for use, even if one only uses it to teach or do research. Some academics can't even do these things well.

But beyond this the kind of intellectuals one might hope would emerge from our schools are those who are concerned with and committed to identifying and solving the problems which plague our personal and social lives. This calls for the creative application of knowledge (transfer, if you wish) to real life. It calls for cognition *plus* affect *plus* action. People who can think with values and commit themselves to action are called intellectuals here. This achievement I assert should be the goal of the schools. If so, the choice appears to rest between educating for an intellectual mentality or training for an academic mind. That the training of academics seems to be the basic intent of most curriculum projects (whether explicit or not) can be seen from the nature of their stated content objectives.

The general thoughtless impulse of the academic to reproduce himself has been greatly aided from within the profession by the occurrence in recent years of two technically facilitating devices. Perhaps the single most influential effort in education along these lines may be found in the two volumes of the *Taxonomy of Educational Objectives: Cognitive and Affective Domains*.[1] A careful reading of these volumes might make one wonder whether youngsters are even supposed to move in school until the taxonomy of motor objectives appears; but more directly the cognitive and affective domains have served as a guidance system for many of the curriculum developments in the past decade.

This is terribly unfortunate and has had, I suggest, rather deleterious effects on education. Although the intent of the taxonomies in "doing their thing" is stated clearly and in good faith, the process by which they were produced and the selection of topics indicates a commitment to and encouragement of the process of training academics.

To begin with, if we are interested in education in behavioral terms, cognitive or otherwise, we certainly do not want to approach it from a measurement mentality (i.e., if you can't measure it, it can't be any good, or it isn't important, or it shouldn't be taught, etc.). There would seem to me to be little other explanation for the planning and development of the taxonomies except for the facilitation of the measurement of educational goals.

Certainly intelligent behavior implies some cognition, some affect and some action: *all together*. Without elements of all three no intelligent behavior could be effected. It is these wholes which ought to be the objectives of education, not lists of separate cognitive or affective or motor potentials. The priority is also quite apparent in this series. The cognitive domain appears first. Does this make it more important? Easier to test? More saleable? Or what?

Surely the authors must know that relatively less attention is paid to that poor cousin, the affective domain, and none to the motor realm, if for no other reason than that they are either less measurable or not stated. It is because the taxonomies are so widely used in curriculum development, because they academically segment people's behavior like frogs on a tray, and because the cognitive domain is obviously given preference that they are dangerous to good education and are irresponsible (at least in retrospect or perhaps in the sense of an "unintended consequence").

The production of the taxonomies is significant evidence of an academic mentality which utilizes technical rationality divorced from consideration of ends. Thus, what can be done and measured becomes what ought to be done. If it isn't evidence of this, then why isn't the taxonomy an integrated statement of the complexities of thought, feeling, and action in the behavior of intelligent people? Perhaps this can't even be catalogued? Or perhaps we would have to wait a few decades?

Little brothers to the taxonomies are what are called behavioral objectives. By this I mean those who have taken the so-called "Tyler" rationale and turned it into a process of grafting or pasting on specific cognitions or affects or actions through a form of behavior modification techniques. The taxonomy offers these people an easy authoritative source to build their "nitty-gritty" programs on. Unfortunately they rarely get beyond the first level of the cognitive domain in any meaningful way. The behavioral-objectives people are in full stride today in many of the curriculum projects and at the local levels. Among other objections to this approach, we might say that they deal mostly in partial segments of human behavior, work best in relation to the most trivial of goals, assume a stance of god-like quality, and, perhaps most dangerously of all, operate from a logic of "means" which is divorced from ends in the logic of the technique.

III. THE ECOLOGY OF CURRICULUM

I suspect that the major problem facing curriculum developers today, if they care about being responsible in the terms discussed here, is that they do not see the curriculum in terms of our modern electronic, computerized, multi-sensory, interrelated, man-made environment. What is needed is an ecological perspective on curriculum.

Without trying to be controversial or raise basic issues about Marshall McLuhan, there is an ecological sense in which we may say that the "medium is the message." Thus, the school as a curriculum medium provides a message which goes far beyond those messages presented by curriculum developers in terms of content. It is an "environment as message" which cannot be said to have a clear, segmented, linear learning payoff.

Furthermore, we do live in a world dominated by mass media and Madison Avenue; we do prepare to send our youngsters to universities at least partially in the service of what the "Movement" people call the military-industrial complex. Even President Eisenhower warned against this alliance of industry, the military, and the scientist in his farewell address.

Youngsters see that knowledge can be a farce; they also see the use we make of education for television advertising. We report to them the results of research on the effects of smoking on the one hand, and present the most enticing advertising in the world to sell cigarettes on the other hand. We further communicate, for example, that the important thing is not what you know, but what grade you get, or at the very least that what you know is only good for taking tests. This is, of course, all part of the ecology of curriculum.

If curriculum developers are concerned about what is learned in contrast to what is presented by the teacher or other materials, media, and/or resource, then the complexity of a dynamic, immediate, multi-sensory world must be faced. The values, assumptions, and facts about human relationships, social roles, functions and uses of the school, the nature of knowledge, and the nature of human nature need to be reflected in the goals and processes of curriculum development.

To assume that some simple linear development model such as

expert to *teacher* to *student* will in any way account for the ecological complexity as it impinges upon student learning is irresponsible or lacking in respond-ability to modern life. Unfortunately most curriculum development still has this single linearity, disguised in some cases by feedback loops and attempts at revision. In contrast to the linear pattern, a circular pattern would at least *begin* to cope with modern curriculum complexities. But this would mean, among other things, seriously involving students in curriculum development, not only through the reports of teachers, but also as active agents in the development. I know of no national curriculum project that has ever seriously entertained this idea.

Thus, curriculum development today is ecologically irresponsible because it pays almost no attention to a number of major factors related to learning: for example, the student, the school as an organization, the reinforcing or contradictory impact of mass media, or the use of knowledge beyond academic tasks. Most curricula are linear, closed, narrow, and unrelated to non-academic life or any of the other aspects of the total school curriculum.

IV. RELEVANCE OF CURRICULUM AND INSTRUCTION AS SEPARATE REALMS

A specific failure or irresponsibility of curriculum developers that is especially relevant to those professionals concerned with the schools is a failure to distinguish between curriculum and instruction, or if you wish, to distinguish two distinct realms of relevant operation.

To me instruction is best described as the activity which takes place primarily in the classroom or some other suitable place under the guidance of someone called a teacher. The curriculum plan is one of the important variables in this setting. Other important variables are the professional quality of the teacher, the personality structures of the teacher and pupils, their personal values, motivation, and past experiences (reflecting their social class origins), as well as peer group pressures. These are all important variables to be considered if we are concerned about pupil *learning* rather than simply teacher or media *presentation*. Curriculum development is simply irresponsible when it does not come to grips with the complexity of variables relevant to instructional practices, or those ecological factors relevant to curriculum planning.

Our ecological perspective should tell us that this is a world of rapidly growing knowledge. It further tells us that almost all the major issues and problems of social and personal significance are moral problems. They are not essentially knowledge issues since we seem sooner or later to be able to do whatever we can imagine in the realm of technology. These social crises do not lend themselves to one-dimensional or single-discipline analyses. Furthermore, our personal problems and feelings, for example, of powerlessness, frustration, and alienation are reflected dramatically in today's contemporary society. Even our faith in democratic procedures is severely threatened.

Now, I submit that presenting a new, up-dated, more authentic, more efficient course in physics, or biology, or mathematics, or you name it will have very little effect on any of the above conditions, whether one has used the taxonomies, behavioral objectives, the structures of the disciplines, or the modes of inquiry.

When our society presents man's hard-won knowledge to the young and represents it as his greatest achievement, only to have our students discover that it does not help them to make sense of the world in terms of themselves or their society, then we are fighting a ridiculously hopeless battle in education, engaging in a true exercise in futility.

The present curricula do not help much because they are related neither to the personal needs and interests of the young, nor to the major social needs and issues of our society and the world, nor even to other parts of the curriculum. This failure, I would assert, is further evidence of irresponsibility.

V. AN ALTERNATIVE MODEL FOR CURRICULUM DEVELOPMENT

We plainly need other models for curriculum development. What follows here is one projection of a possibility. This model, to be adequate, would certainly include all of the following items:

1. A circular rather than a linear pattern of development, including experts, professional educators, schoolmen and teachers, parents, and students as meaningful and fully contributing members in the process of curriculum development.

2. Goals and objectives that centered on behavior, reflecting a focus upon the integration of thinking, feeling, and acting in human behavior.

3. A continuous process of development.

4. An organization of curriculum content and of human relations in the school such that knowledge could be related to one's self, to society, and to other areas of knowledge.

5. Evaluation reflecting the aesthetic and ethical qualities of living together in schools rather than emphasizing the technical measurement mentality and its related grading-and-categorizing syndrome, evaluation which focused its technical efforts upon the "payoff" area — the use of student competencies to create a more fruitful and productive personal and social life through the release of human capacities.

This alternative suggests that curriculum developers, if they are to be responsible, must face up to the complexity of the task and must commit themselves to studying the arrangement of the relationships of such factors in specific contexts.

Let us explore this alternative by the use of a simple figure. In comparison to the linearity in the development process suggested by A in Figure 1, we move to the circular arrangement suggested by B in Figure 1.

The linear section (A in Figure 1) is based primarily upon a technical rationale. This rationale on the curriculum level refers to identifying content to be taught, specifying the scope, sequence, and activities (or experiences) to be provided, and projecting an evaluation design. On the instructional level this rationale is specifically defined by stating objectives (often behavioral), selecting and organizing experiences, and evaluating. These are essentially phases which begin with objectives (often screened for evaluative potential) or bodies of content with inherent goals embedded in them.

Section B, circularity, is intended to indicate a process whereby all relevant participants take part in curriculum development in a much more dynamic fashion.

Differences in the two approaches may be seen, for example, in terms of the inclusion of participants deemed relevant to curriculum development and their role, the character of the goals, and the bases utilized for organizing the content and processes.

The linear model originates with objectives and/or content supplied, essentially, by the scholar-expert. This is translated into curriculum plans (activities, patterns, evaluative means, etc.) with

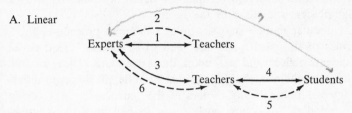

Figure 1.

Linear and Circular Curriculum Development Models

A. Linear

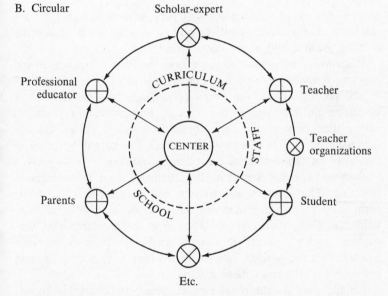

B. Circular

the help of some teachers via the first feedback loop. A different group of selected teachers then try out the plans with students, from whom the teacher gets feedback which in turn is fed back to the scholar-expert. The data fed back relates primarily to the achievement of the content objectives in the context of the activities and patterns, and the abilities, of a given population of students.

The goals sought and evaluated are primarily "inside" a special discipline and they are almost entirely stated and evaluated in cognitive terms. The relevance of the material is almost entirely inner coherence within the discipline with little or no relevance to personal meaning, social problems, or other disciplines. Once the technical "pattern" has run its course, the curriculum plans are complete for a period of time. Up-dating will take place by a similar process sometime in the future.

The circular model[2] suggests quite a different procedure. First, the roles of the participants are seen to be "equal." That is, all participants reflect and act upon the same data. They are not specialized links in a chain, links that do different things at different times. The organizing centers of the "curriculum" (the circle in the middle) are continuously being shaped by a more immediate, multi-participant interaction. This in effect means the intrusion into the planning process of personally meaningful student interests, parental community concerns, special needs of specific cultural groups, and major social problems.

Responsible curriculum development means that all participants must be accessible to each other in order to have "respond-ability" in the process. Thus, for example, students and parents would be in on the dialogue at the level of the curriculum planning, rather than only in the instructional activity. It should be immediately clear that objectives and plans formulated by scholars can only be one aspect of the planning process.

It should also be clear that all participants need accessibility to planning. This kind of accessibility will demand that the basic form used to organize planning must be meaningful to all participants. Thus, disciplines of knowledge as unrelated and segmented academic specializations cannot be the basic form, since neither students, parents, nor many teachers have access through previous experience to these disciplines.

On the contrary the scholar-expert must contribute his knowledge and judgment to something to which the other participants can also contribute their knowledge and judgment. This suggests that the form of the curriculum content will of necessity be focused upon large, inter-disciplinary loadings of knowledge built around major inter-disciplinary ideas and/or basic social themes.

A number of possibilities may be presented. Certainly the concept of "systems" has great generative inter-disciplinary power. Further, the social themes of technology, mass media, and/or communication, the world of work, industrialization, and urbanization, etc., are fruitful areas.

The crucial factor here is really not the specific organizing centers, per se; one would agree to a certain arbitrariness in any of them. The important criteria of selection are, rather, the abilities of a selected "center" to integrate the variety of planners, disciplines, and levels of potential student accomplishment under a common roof.

Pupil accomplishment itself would be focused on broader "objectives" than the specific cognitive concepts and/or facts that can be generated and tied into a common theme. Much more attention would need to be paid to processes for developing thinking, valuing, communicating, social relating, and utilizing materials, and to ways of inquiring, studying, and finding data. These processes of finding and using data for developing personal, functional, transferable competencies would become the heart of the curriculum.

The shift in evaluation would then bring it into line with these more appropriate educational goals. Aesthetic and moral criteria which focus upon the quality of living experiences in the process of encountering the curriculum would become a large part of our evaluation concerns.

The basic instructional evaluation question would thus become: Does the curriculum create conditions for learning which result in student freedom, choice, awareness of alternatives, self-directed activity, perseverance in pursuit of goals, enthusiasm and vitality in action, and completion with a sense of satisfaction of self-defined tasks?

Feedback to planners would focus upon evaluating the curriculum in terms of such questions as these: Are teachers and students able to utilize the organizing centers productively? Are there enough materials available for different student interests and levels of accomplishment? Are there evidences of behavior such as thinking, valuing, communicating, social relating, finding, and using data?

The process of developing the curriculum would necessitate an emphasis upon the role of a functioning catalyst, integrator, and/or synthesizer. At the moment it would appear that the curriculum director is the best candidate for this responsibility. The curriculum director (and staff) would by necessity become a curriculum scholar-in-residence in the school system. The special kinds of concerns that professional people in curriculum have would now become primary integrating foci for planning. I refer, of course, to problems such as balance and integration in the curriculum, continuity in the experience of youngsters, and the welding together of knowledge, teachers, parents, and students into meaningful and satisfying programs.

The organization of this process would be fraught with problems. Ideally, it would be of maximum advantage to have inter-disciplinary teams of scholars on part-time loan from universities at all times, engaging in a curriculum *conversation* with parents, students, teachers, and professional educators. This conversation would be integrated by the activity of curriculum personnel and by the categories of inter-disciplinary, socially, and personally relevant concerns, all focused upon the processing behavior of students and the moral and aesthetic conditions for maximal living and learning.

Short of this ideal, a variety of phasing procedures could be used which involved persons representative of all groups in meaningful discourse in the planning process. If flexibility, generality, and common centers characterized all planning activities, then each group could enter into some participant role.

VI. A PARTIAL EXEMPLAR

A program partially modeled on the exemplar suggested above is being carried out by the Curriculum Laboratory at Goldsmith's College, University of London.[3] Emphasis has been upon the instructional level with only occasional forays into the realm of curriculum planning. The program is called *Interdisciplinary Enquiry*. It is focused upon the creation of teams of teachers in English secondary schools representing a number of different disciplines (the actual participation is voluntary). Teams consist of from three to six teachers, most often from the areas of social studies, English, and the arts, but occasionally including science or mathematics members.

The teams get together and select a large theme or problem as an organizing center. Some of those I worked with included "communication," "the world of work," and "technology." Teachers then organized pools of resources around their selected themes, and projected plans for what are called "starters." These starters are essentially initiating stimulus sessions which immerse the students in the theme and give them some awareness of alternative areas for inquiry.

Once students begin to develop some interest, the teachers facilitate the formation of inquiry groups and/or individual inquiries. Plans are made and students begin to pursue their special interest, with the teacher acting as a resource and a process facilitator. Teachers work with groups that fall most into their own areas of competency (not always just academic competency), and this choice is usually a voluntary one.

The general process of inquiry continues with re-stimulation, planning, doing, making, and reporting until the students and teachers begin to sense and agree that the process has begun to dry up. Great emphasis is, of course, placed upon active student inquiring and making activity. Usually this program amounts to about 40 per cent of the total program, with other times allotted for remedial work, autonomous subjects (usually mathematics and foreign languages), and special elective studies or disciplines.

This program (IDE) falls far short of the curriculum development model proposed above in that most of its efforts have been concerned with the instructional level. Many of the weaknesses which have been noted by evaluators grew out of the failure to integrate the community and scholar-experts into the process.[4] The students, of course, had a much more active role than usual, but were still not completely involved. In other words this approach leans more toward the "grass roots" model.

The program *is* instructive, however, in that many of the weaknesses and needs noted suggest procedures similar to those projected in the previous model. Certainly the identification of viable themes and the preparation of resource pools would be greatly facilitated by the circular model of development.

VII. CONCLUSION

In closing I would like to reiterate my feeling that our present curriculum development procedures are irresponsible (i.e., lack respond-ability); that one major culprit in this failure is the development of a technical logic applied to segmented objectives; and that the developmental processes are not appropriate for the ecology of curriculum reality. In place of these things, I suggest a more dynamic circular model involving the integration of disciplines, people, and participation.

REFERENCES

[1] Benjamin S. Bloom, (ed.) *Taxonomy of Educational Objectives, Handbook I: Cognitive Domain,* New York: David McKay and Co., 1956; David R. Krathwohl, Benjamin S. Bloom, Bertram B. Masia, *Taxonomy of Educational Objectives, Handbook II: Affective Domain,* New York: David McKay and Co., 1964.

[2] The alternative being suggested should not be confused with the "grass roots" model of curriculum development. The grass roots model leaned heavily on teacher initiation and direction without giving other legitimate participants a role to play. While the linear model is a "top-down" procedure, the grass roots model is more like a "bottom-up" pattern. The circular model is intended to suggest a dynamic and interactive model involving all at a common level.

[3] I was Visiting Professor there, working in the Curriculum Laboratory, during the 1967–68 school year.

[4] J. B. Macdonald and Sam Manger, "A Study of an Interdisciplinary Enquiry Curriculum" Mimeographed, School of Education, University of Wisconsin-Milwaukee, Milwaukee, Wis. 1969.

Richard E. Schutz

Comments on

RESPONSIBLE

CURRICULUM DEVELOPMENT

The first reading of Professor Macdonald's paper elicited recollections of the initial lecture in my first class in the psychology of learning under Professor John Seward many years ago. Dr. Seward stated that the course would be concerned with the question, "What happens when a person learns something?" An immediate reaction from a then would-be world-saver, now a responsible research scientist, was "That's not too difficult. A person works at something that he can't do for a while, and then he gradually gets the hang of it. It happens all the time." "Fine," said Seward, "and just how does he happen to get the hang of it?" "Ah, that's very difficult to say," acknowledged the student. "All right," said Seward, "might we consider that question for a while?" We have yet to formulate a satisfactory answer. Curriculum appears to constitute an analogous problem, and manipulating the rubrics surrounding the concept does not simplify the empirical problems associated with it.

Macdonald's paper is representative of a growing academic tendency to use confession of guilt and verbal self-flagellation as a prelude to passing moral judgment on the institutions and ideas which are viewed as determinants of the unfortunate status that has been defined. Although I share completely Macdonald's objectives of attaining more perfect human conditions, I find myself sanguine where he is discouraged and pessimistic where he is optimistic.

I am impressed by Macdonald's rhetoric. I've certainly never considered curriculum developments as "technical one-dimensional arrows shot into the school situation [which] rupture the educational process and reduce it to bloody rivulets of . . . passive conformity." The images produced by this rhetoric are something I'd expect to experience on a bad trip, but not while reading a professional paper. Part of my difficulty comes in identifying clear referents for responsibility or the lack thereof in this context. Conceptualizing irresponsible persons is no problem; conceptualizing irresponsible events or other clearly bounded things such as taxonomies is possible; but conceptualizing unbounded complexes such as developmental processes and intellectual tools boggles my mind.

Rhetoric aside, it is common knowledge that we are currently unable "to account adequately for the major variables and kinds of persons rightfully involved in the phenomenological context of schooling." Since this is Macdonald's definition of responsibility, I suppose I should plead *mea culpa* and roll Macdonald's hoop model of curriculum development twice around the altar in penance. Rather, I shall further implicate myself by rejecting the assumptions Professor Macdonald presents in his introductory remarks. Setting up mutually exclusive categories of humanities versus sciences, logic of aesthetic disciplines versus scientific disciplines, synthesis versus analysis, and assigning education consistently to the former appears to me to be irresponsible under Macdonald's definition of the term. Moreover, the assumptions appear to be a verbal frosting; they provide a rhetorical but not a deductive base for Macdonald's position. A more reasonable motivation for Macdonald's chief points is Norman Storer's view of education as a conjoint discipline which increments knowledge from many traditional disciplines, in contrast to Macdonald's view of education as a traditional discipline which generates knowledge about itself.

Macdonald appears to be heavily influenced by the currently popular academic religion which seeks the three R's — responsibility, relevance, and revolution — all via adjustments of the symbolic rather than the empirical environment. Given a choice, most people would opt for "sensitive and emergent happenings" in contrast to "built-in rigidity." But to consider *verbal* options as isomorphic to *empirical* options is dangerous. Present problems in the schools are seriously aggravated, not ameliorated, by an academic tendency to lyricize problems rather than to operationalize solutions.

Although Macdonald may feel comfortable in dealing with metaphors rather than cause-effect chains, the man on the street as well as the student on the campus is demonstrating vividly that he considers this an irresponsible professional position. Neither is the time-worn professional lament concerning "the obvious inability to evaluate the outcomes of schooling in large-scale social terms or long-range personal terms" any longer acceptable. The man on the street can, and is, performing such evaluation easily and is finding the performance low. Moreover, he is becoming more articulate in publicizing his evaluative results and is also finding mechanisms to exercise accountability checks to raise the performance level. Since he operates in real time, there are empirical consequences associated with the analysis, which responsible curriculum developers are well advised to respect.

Rather than facing the implications of any one of the current crises in education squarely, Macdonald is inclined to tilt his sword at windmills of the mind, doing battle with the taxonomies, the measurement mentality, the academic mentality, and behavioral objectives. This begs the question of responsibility. Irrespective of its conceptual strength or weakness, to suggest that the *Taxonomy of Educational Objectives* is either a technically facilitating device or that it has had "deleterious effects on education" is theological cant. Let's face it. Neither the taxonomy nor any other manipulable variable has had any *demonstrable* effect, deleterious or facilitating, on observable educational outcomes. We simply have not yet acquired the necessary knowledge to reliably promote or extinguish changes in individuals through education, or in educational institutions through societal structures. But to charge educators with professional irresponsibility in the light of this state of affairs is no more warranted than to charge irresponsibility in medicine because cancer is not now curable or irresponsibility in engineering because the moon is not now inhabited.

Tolerance of performance that falls short of omniscience and omnipotence is a human courtesy conventionally extended to professionals in curriculum development as members of the species. Persons concerned with educational improvement are as eligible for this courtesy as anyone else. It is not at all inconsistent to present "man's hard-won knowledge . . . as his greatest achievement" and at the same time admit that we still do not know how to eliminate "feelings of powerlessness, frustration, or alienation." It is unnecessary that the young should find this discovery traumatic and unreasonable or that accountable professionals should conclude that we are thereby "fighting a ridiculously hopeless battle." Windmills can be turned as well as stabbed. To fail to recognize the distinction is a dangerous human condition.

Rejecting the possibility of an objective curriculum "out there," Macdonald forfeits a good deal of human experience. The separation of symbolic representation from object-phenomenon is a distinctly human characteristic. Without the distinction, Macdonald has no alternative but to confound the squiggles he makes on paper with squiggling learners. I submit that it makes no whit of difference to the squiggling student whether a paradigm is drawn using straight or closed-curved lines. The only effect is on persons responding directly to the paradigm. Macdonald's paradigm has curious consequences for him. For example, he recommends eliminating all division of labor among students, teachers, parents, professional educators, and scholar-experts — with teacher organizations and *et cetera* formally thrown in for good measure. It would take a superhuman "functioning catalyst" to assemble and manage such a set of individuals for any prolonged period of time.

Macdonald's description of his implementation of the paradigm indicates that it has yet to be tested. The only persons in the instructional act in the Interdisciplinary Enquiry Curriculum are teachers and students, and the focus is still on the conceptual framework of knowledge. The framing of knowledge around "inter-disciplinary ideas and/or basic social themes" is likely to lead to a high degree of superficiality.

While I find Macdonald's analysis of the determinants of the present impotence of curriculum development unconvincing and his suggestions for improvement unmanageable, the general problem Macdonald addresses is not to be ignored. Macdonald perceptively recognizes that curriculum development technology is primitive. However, persons and agencies who have been concerned with adding to this technology rather than damning it have made rapid strides in the last three to five years. Thus, the view of curriculum development reflected in the projects Macdonald uses for Brand X illustrations lags behind the current state-of-the-art of instructional development technology.

Extending instructional development technology has meant treating *empirically* such constructs as ecology, media, and multi-disciplinary relationships which Macdonald insightfully identifies as having been ignored. It also requires attention to political, economic, sociological, anthropological, business, and engineering knowledge and techniques which have not heretofore been brought to bear on education. Even the aesthetic and moral disciplines which Macdonald touts are beginning to make a definite, modest contribution.

These knowledge systems are not tapped in "the total context of our curriculum needs and problems." Improvements in other human services such as health and transportation have been achieved on a *specific,* rather than a general scale. In these fields the concern for totality is aimed not at the problem level but at the solution level. A total solution to a problem of whatever size is useful; a total problem without a solution remains a problem irrespective of how finely it may be analyzed. In abrogating suboptimal improvement because it is inferior to optimal improvement, education has remained totally unimproved. I'm using the term improvement here to include the conventional criteria of utility, dependability, time, and cost.

Alternative strategies for achieving the goals of Macdonald's practical arts approach are available which give equal priority to human interdependency but concurrently provide a means of differentiating accountability and dividing authority in the relationships. To illustrate one alternative, I shall draw on the experience of the Southwest Regional Laboratory, using as referents a programmatic development endeavor directed to produce the instructional wherewithal to teach reading to young children at a high level of dependability. We have carefully specified and sequenced a lexicon and identified the desired behavioral operations the child will be able to perform on this lexicon. The development task is to provide the methods and materials which enable him to perform these operations through activities that he will find attractive and those responsible for the instruction will find manageable.

Prevailing instructional practice is based upon a simple diad of teacher and learner. Other personnel such as remedial specialists are occasionally involved. Parents, too, are occasionally brought into the network but typically to assist in remedial efforts also. The Laboratory network utilizes this diad as a key element. No effort is made to avoid or remove the teacher. Neither is there any expectation that a product will be "teacher-proof" or "pupil-proof." Effort is directed toward strengthening and supporting the diad by expanding the resources that are made available to it.

At the learner-contact level the network is augmented by specific provision for parents and tutors. Procedures and materials have been prepared for teachers to use in describing learner objectives and activities to parents. Reporting procedures have been developed for reporting outcome attainment to parents, and "homework" has been prepared which requires the assistance of parents or other members of the family and which the teacher and parents may decide is relevant. A kit of activities and exercises is also available for use by parents during summer to maintain the strength of attained skills during the vacation period.

Procedures and materials have been prepared for use by student

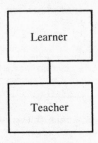

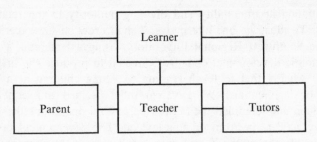

tutors. To date, the Laboratory has worked with fifth- and sixth-grade youngsters as tutors, but older persons with comparable skills could as easily perform the function. The materials and methods used by the tutors are designed to require minimal special skills and to make maximum use of general human skills. Materials are also available for use by a teacher or principal to train a cadre of tutors.

At the teacher-contact level a different kind of resource is represented. The network distinguishes three components. The line of administration running from principal to superintendent includes persons with direct administrative authority and responsibility. Staff services are categorized into two components. Supervisory service personnel include the age-grade and/or subject-matter structured curriculum supervisors. Pupil personnel service staff include guidance and counseling and related support services. At the present time, Laboratory-developed materials and procedures for this level include briefing information about the program,

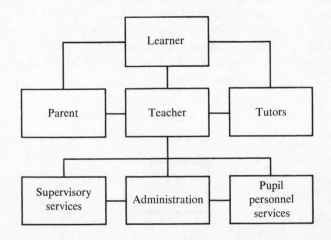

procedures for providing these personnel with pupil performance data in a form they find manageable and useful, and materials which can be used for their staff and public information purposes. Since the development of system support at this level is at an early stage and will be expanded within the next year, it is anticipated that further requirements will be identified.

It is evident that the network moves from involvement of individuals at the instructional level to the involvement of staff groups at the support level and to the involvement of institutions at the agency level. SWRL constitutes a development agency; a local educational unit constitutes a monitoring agency; another laboratory, a state or intermediate educational unit, or a supplementary educational center might constitute a monitoring support agency. Each component of the network has clearly defined responsibilities for promoting or verifying learner achievement of the desired outcomes of the instructional programs.

It is apparent that this functional network generates a different view of human resource utilization in education. The consequences of this view are far-reaching, with implications for teacher training, in-service training, teaching and administrative responsibility, parent and community involvement, and manpower planning. When the implications have been worked out, it will be possible

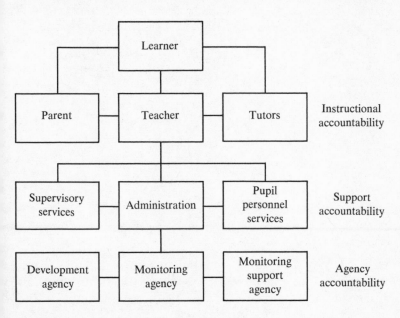

"to account adequately for the major variables and kinds of persons rightfully involved in the phenomenological context of schooling." Moreover, the chief advantage of the strategy is that it permits an objective assessment of the cumulative progress toward this goal, assigning accountability and acknowledging accomplishment commensurate with responsible curriculum development.

SIX

ROBERT G. HANVEY

THE SOCIAL STUDIES, THE EDUCATIONAL CULTURE, THE STATE

The title of this paper is pretentious. I apologize, but not very much. First, in speaking of the social studies it seems appropriate to be pretentious. The social studies embraces everything in sight, with very little warmth and absolutely no virility.

Actually, the title is reasonably precise. If we have learned anything from the work of the national curriculum projects it is that the improvement of curriculum cannot be isolated from larger structural problems inherent in the culture of the schools. The reason for including "the state" in the title is more obscure. One part of the answer is that the school serves as the agent of the state, implicitly and explicitly orienting itself to national interests, to economic needs and political traditions structured on national lines. This fact has a special meaning for the social studies, which numbers among its many claims a particular responsibility for citizenship education.

But let me back away from the grandiose and begin with the merely morose. If you go, randomly, into a hundred high school social studies classrooms today you will almost certainly depart from ninety of them with a feeling of depression. Whether this holds true for other subjects I don't know. After a six- or seven-year flurry of curriculum reform activity, it still holds true for the social studies. Six or seven years, of course, is not a long time. One might argue and hope that when the work of all the various curriculum projects in the social studies has come to the point of widespread commercial distribution significant changes will begin to be evident. This is possible, just as it is possible that in the next election Mississippi will vote overwhelmingly for the Socialist-Labor candidate. But the pilot tests of new materials do not really support such a hope.

Let's go back a few years to a time when a more simple optimism prevailed. What did the reformers think was wrong with the traditional programs in social studies and what did they propose to do about it? The indictment read something like the following: "Lifeless, irrelevant, formal rather than real and behavioral, text-bound. And fearful. Afraid to touch certain tabooed topics." Some of the critics — and I was one — felt that the central problem lay in the fact that the social studies was history-dominated, and not by scholarly history, but by a conventionalized, blatantly ethnocentric history.

Many of us felt that the solution lay in introducing the social sciences into pre-college education. Until this time the social sciences lived on very short rations indeed in pre-college education. Various individuals, following the lead of colleagues in the natural sciences and mathematics, obtained the sponsorship of professional associations and applied for federal monies to support curriculum projects. The Anthropology Curriculum Study Project was the first social science project supported by the National Science Foundation. Later, the Foundation supported the geographers and sociologists in similar endeavors. The United States Office of Education supported a wider range of reform efforts, most of them not tied so tightly to specific disciplines.

The projects saw their task as one of developing materials and methods. The materials were to represent the best scholarship in their respective fields but were to be planned for use in the context of a more inductive pedagogy.

Several of the social science projects faced a somewhat different problem than did the curriculum projects in other subjects. There was no ready-made niche in school programs. There was no old anthropology course to replace with a new one. So, considerable attention was given in the early days to a strategy of insinuation — how in the world to even get in the school door. The geographers didn't face this problem but the sociologists and the anthropologists did. The sociologists had a slight advantage in that elective courses in sociology had been offered in American high schools for a half-century. Anthropology, on the other hand, had simply never had a place.

The strategy that we finally elected was chosen because it looked as though it might work, because it was consistent with our definition of the faults of the traditional social studies, and because it made sense in terms of what anthropology as a discipline had to offer. We decided to subvert a course very commonly taught in the ninth or tenth grade — the world history course. More specifically, we intended to offer materials that could be rationalized as world history and which would, in effect, substitute for a substantial segment of the traditional course. Many supporters of anthropology in the high schools urged us to design a high school level anthropology course. We resisted this advice; we knew that such a program would never become a required course and we knew what happened to elective courses. The elective route was no way to bring large numbers of students into a meaningful encounter with anthropology.

But with what kind of anthropology was this to be an encounter? School people had some rather definite expectations. They had read Mead and Montague, Benedict and Kroeber. They knew that anthropologists studied primitives and dug up old bones and stones. Many hoped for something exotic on savages, something appropriately liberal on race, something fascinating on the archeological search for lost civilizations. Some of the interest was not at this level. Many teachers knew that anthropologists have a sovereign interest in the idea of culture and they felt that this was an idea that might have great utility in social analysis. In general, the appeal of anthropology to school people seemed to rest on a mix of attitudes and sentiments: a sympathy for cultural relativism, a *National Geographic* kind of fascination with far-off places and primitive peoples, a sophisticated search for more useful kinds of analytic ideas.

The project staff listened to these ideas and read them; most projects receive a heavy flow of correspondence. In the end, we catered to them only slightly. It isn't that we ignored the wishes of the schools in favor of the wishes of the scholars. We were selective in our response to both groups. What the scholars urged on us was often foolishly technical and specialized. There are not many anthropologists in the United States. We have had contact with a substantial number of them. Some advised us well, that is, in a direction we liked. Some advised us badly, that is, in a direction we thought unprofitable. In the end we chose to treat certain topics that were unrepresented, under-represented or badly represented in high school programs.

One of these topics is human evolution. The biologists in their new curriculum treated biological evolution of animals very comprehensively but said very little of importance about human evolution. Human evolution is not just biological evolution. It is also cultural evolution and much of the theorizing has to do with the feedback relationships between culture and morphology — the relationship, for example, between teeth and tools. The little Australopithecus of two million years ago had already lost the large canines which serve as anatomical weapons; this loss strongly suggests that he had been using non-anatomical means of defense for a very long time. In any event, our main interest is in the evolution of humanness, of the human system of adaptation. That system includes anatomical, psychological, and sociological components. What evolved, we emphasize, was not just a particular anatomical creature but a total, articulated, and most importantly open-ended system of adaptation that includes childhood dependency, the family, erect posture, continual sexual interest, the neurological capacity for language, rule-bound rather than instinct-bound behavior, etc.

As an example of how selective we were in responding to the advice of anthropologists and to the traditions of anthropology, consider how we handled magic. Magic is a favorite gambit of anthropologists. Most ethnographies report on magic and religion; it is one of the traditional categories of observation and analysis. Much of the anthropological description of magic has to do with magical practice, magical acts. We put magic into a different context. At the end of four weeks of laboratory problems on human evolution, we ask a summarizing question: What hath evolution wrought? What was the product of several million years of change? The answer we hope for, as indicated above, is that the final product is a complex system of adaptation. One element in that system is magical thought. Magical thought is pervasive in the human species, as common in "advanced" societies as in primitive. Presumably magical thought was functional within the adaptive system or at least not so dysfunctional as to be selected against. The question we pose to students is this: What might be the adaptive utility of a tendency to engage in magical thinking? We proceed by analyzing beliefs in ghosts and witches and we ask students to consider the possible advantages and disadvantages, psychological and sociological, of such beliefs. We have some tentative explanations in mind and we eventually make them known, explicitly emphasizing their tentative nature. These explanations require that students understand the ideas of "projection" and "displacement." So these ideas are introduced.

Most anthropologists would not have advised us in this direction. In fact, when we asked for help on this matter it turned out that no one had yet written specifically to these questions, although a few were beginning to venture in this direction.

In any event, human evolution and human nature were topics we felt to be very under-represented in high school education and we have given them a substantial role in our materials. The final product after years of development and classroom testing of materials in seventy schools is a one-semester course called Patterns in Human History. There are four parts to the course. The first part has to do with how one studies human societies, the second with the origins and nature of humanness, the third with the emergence of more complex human societies — tribes and states — after the food-producing revolution, and the fourth centers on peasant societies and the modernization of peasant societies.

The course we have developed is not a diluted college anthropology course. It is something entirely new and has, we think, a justifiable place in secondary school social studies. Given the commitment of the schools to programs in history, we have more history to offer than anyone. Everyone but anthropologists neglects the first 99 per cent of human history as if it didn't matter.

As with courses developed by other projects, Patterns in Human History is rich in data. And pains have been taken to present the data in ways that suit the high school classroom. If you are truly determined to be effective you end up with something that educators are fond of calling "multi-media," that is, filmstrips, records, overhead transparencies, evidence cards, and casts, as well as readings. Each component has years of classroom testing behind it. And the history of each component includes a lot of bad guesses and, often, terrifying costs. But sufficient funds gave the projects the luxury of admitting their faults and the opportunity to correct them.

In general the social science projects, like the other national curriculum projects, did a good job of producing materials. In most instances the materials were clearly superior to those found in many college classrooms. At every national meeting of anthropologists we are approached by college teachers who beg to obtain the instructional materials that have been developed for high school use. But good materials, it turned out, were not enough.

Let's come back to the schools. The projects saw their mission as one of devising a new curriculum "diet." That was a limited, focused task. In undertaking it, the projects accepted the habits and lifeways of the schools pretty much as they were. In effect they said, if you will use the new diet as directed you'll feel much better. The schools, of course, didn't use as directed. They poured it into their ears, smeared it on their bodies, and burned it as incense — and felt marvelously improved.

That was the first jolt — the continual reporting of success when every observation showed no success. But this wasn't too hard to explain. Anything was better than what had gone before. And then, too, reform was in the air; people expected new things to be better things.

There were other jolts, more serious ones. Even with highly recommended teachers, there was often a serious lack of precision in the handling of ideas. This might suggest that the problem was a lack of formal training in anthropology, a not unreasonable hypothesis. We didn't provide formal training, even in the form of workshops. Nor did we require it. Our strategy was for the teacher to learn on the job, with the help of a detailed teaching plan. Such a strategy might easily result in faulty command of important ideas. But, unfortunately, another shock was that teachers not trained in anthropology did generally better than those who had received formal training. Something else was at work.

There were other developments, not always as surprising. It became clear after a few years that for many teachers the receptivity to our materials was based not on any thirst for anthropology but on the inquiry-orientation of the materials. Substantive ideas were a less important consideration than method.

Eventually — much too slowly — we realized that we were

dealing not with isolated phenomena but with a total cultural system, the culture of the schools. The surprises and shocks were the same as those experienced by naive Peace Corps volunteers. The schools are swamps and the people in them have learned to live in the swamp. The naive reformers thought they could improve things by replacing thatched roofs with tin ones. Unfortunately, that still left the swamp and the reformers got wet right up to their eyebrows.

The culture of the schools is a beautifully articulated system. It has these traits: (1) an unbelievably heavy work load for teachers, (2) professional norms that call for innovation in methods and in the organization of curriculum but that do not demand intellectual behavior, (3) almost total lack of discussion of substantive ideas within the faculty, (4) a lack of critical feedback from colleagues or supervisors, and (5) a continual call for harmony within the faculty group.

Certain projects — ours among them — went into the schools expecting to bring about a high level of intellectual performance on the part of teachers and students. But teachers are not expected to be intellectuals. Many are capable, but the whole system is organized in another direction. The work load does not permit the teacher to reflect, to read, to be even a consumer of current scholarship; and what the work load does not permit, the role does not expect.

As a trade-off for the work burden and the modest rewards, teachers are provided with a high degree of job security. Such a role ultimately selects individuals willing for one reason or another to accept such an exchange. Part of the tacit arrangement is the unwritten rule that there will be minimal evaluation of teachers by professional colleagues or superiors. Teachers can go on year after year saying utterly ridiculous things to their classes. There is no complaint, no feedback. And there are no arrangements for dropping intellectually inadequate or lazy teachers.

Since substantive intellectual performance is not a criterion of teacher performance, other things become important. Innovation in itself is a criterion of effective performance. And the system requires only superficial evidence of innovation. In fact, it is doubtful that the system can tolerate genuinely profound innovation.

One of the interesting aspects of all this is the implication for teacher training. The schools *and* the projects have had what can only be called a magical belief in teacher training. But training in substantive ideas doesn't tidily resolve the problem of intellectual imprecision. There is a need for an intellectual climate, for continual intellectual activity (and even abrasiveness). And teacher training doesn't get at the lack of a feedback system that continually holds a mirror up to teaching performance. Teacher training is the defensive recourse of a bureaucratic system. It's something that one does to the lowest level functionary and that can be expected not to send tremors through the whole structure.

So far I haven't said anything about school culture as bureaucratic culture. But this, of course, is what I've been describing: a system in which it is possible to survive without success, a system where idiosyncratic talents are a danger to the security and harmony of the group and where a passive acceptance of hierarchy is valued above all else. The passivity of teachers comes across very strongly as one observes the schools. Vernon Haubrich of the University of Wisconsin identifies the following as the personal characteristics consonant with life in bureaucratic organizations: loyalty, acceptance of seniority, conviviality, and especially dependency. This fits.

The bureaucratic setting for curriculum reform was not given serious attention in the early years of the projects. However, this situation has changed and efforts have been directed to specific aspects of the problem. Teacher training, for example, is no longer viewed with the same simple faith as the means to an improved program. The development of feedback systems for teachers has assumed some importance, but more important, attempts have been made to sensitize administrators to the consequences of bureaucratic rigidity. Among some project people, at least, there has been interest in bringing pressure to bear on the problem of the teacher's work load. The new materials imply new standards of teacher performance and it has become clear that those standards cannot become operational independently of other changes. Helping the teacher become more autonomous rather than "teacher-proofing" the materials makes sense, because the evidence is that you can't teacher-proof the materials.

How will the new social science programs fare over the coming years? Most of the programs are just on the verge of commercial distribution and a firm answer will have to wait. Several new programs, less strictly tied to the social science disciplines, are doing very well. They have the advantage of being first on the market, they are in the inquiry mode, and the student materials are lively and interesting.

How the more strictly social-science-oriented programs fare over the coming years will depend partly, I would argue, on changes in our general sophistication as a society, and especially on changes in our view of the state. There is a basic tension, I would propose, between the latent functions of the social sciences and the latent functions of the traditional social studies. The schools are agents of the state and they have served the state, but in ways that are not generally recognized. In order to explain, let me talk for a moment about the "state" in its most generic sense.

The state is a relatively new form of human society — only about six thousand years old. It is distinguished by its capacity to integrate large, heterogeneous populations and is characterized by a radically asymmetrical distribution of power and wealth. That is to say, power is highly centralized and there are well-developed social classes. It is a highly unstable form of society, as much of what we conventionally call history attests. Much of its instability derives from its asymmetrical distributions. There have been repeated attempts over the centuries to work out more satisfying human relationships within the context of a large-scale state organization. The history of the Western world over the last five hundred years can be read as a succession of efforts to reduce the asymmetries, to redistribute power and wealth and to build institutions that guard against future concentrations of these goods.

These efforts tend to achieve, at best, very modest success. Extreme differentials in material goods and in power seem to be common characteristics of the state and this is as true of modern, industrial states as it is of traditional states.

The persistent problem that states face because of asymmetrical distributions is how to hold the society together. States depend on various institutional and symbolic means to forestall or contain dissatisfaction with prevailing differentials in the allocation of goods and values. In traditional states, religion has been the major instrument of legitimization. In modern states, the schools and the mass media have taken the place of religious institutions as indoctrinative and legitimizing agencies. But although the schools and the media serve to some extent as stabilizing influences, they also — in part wittingly and in part unwittingly — can act as unsettling influences. The schools and the media are locked into the system, but their own organizational values and imperatives give them a certain autonomy and power, and in the exercise of that power they have the potentiality of supplying the intellectual and informational basis for dissatisfaction. In our times this potentiality has been realized by the media but not to any extent by the schools. The schools have served the state not through what they taught by through what was *not* taught. The important curriculum in the social studies has been a null curriculum. The social studies has as its announced mission citizenship education. The most important aspect of citizenship education in American schools — admitted by everyone and by every study — is its utter emptiness and sterility.

The latent function, then, of the traditional social studies has been to preclude the possibility of certain learnings and certain intellectual postures. The primary way in which the social studies and the schools have served the state is by never entertaining the idea that the nation-state might itself be looked at as an object, as a temporary and mutable human phenomenon.

Some of the new social science materials lean in this direction and when that intent is recognized they will quite rightly be perceived as dangerous by many educators. The schools live in a highly political environment and are in a precarious position. It is not that the schools are not prepared to discuss already defined social issues. They are. In fact, training for partisan debate is one of the things in which they delight. But dealing with overt issues is safer than coping with cultural assumptions. An unearthed assumption is not always a pretty sight. The schools are not really braced for that kind of revelation. The most carefully buried assumption of all is the primacy and legitimacy and value of the nation-state. Any policy is home safe when it is defended in terms of the national interests. The highest good of all is presumed to be the well-being of the national society.

Suppose the new social science programs succeeded. Suppose they were taught well and many students — not just a few — came out of the high schools with less passive views of authority, students demanding evidence, able to discern cultural assumptions, politically sophisticated. Consider the problems for a nation so favored. Can a state make its way in the international environment if it cannot count on a large number of docile, essentially uneducated young men who defer to authority and who can be easily persuaded of the legitimacy of national policies and actions. Nations act amorally and justify themselves in moral terms. But if high school graduates were truly educated the justifications would be easily penetrated. The fundamental question is: Can a nation survive if its young people are well educated?

This is an outrageous question, of course. Largely because it is so academic. Experimental curricula which have yet to demonstrate their capacity to subvert so minor an institution as world history courses are not very likely to end up by subverting the national society. The more likely turn of events is that the social sciences will eventually be tolerated in the schools because that national society is becoming more sophisticated, because it has somewhat blindly but effectively worked out new kinds of social adhesive, quite adequate to the task of resisting the possible centrifugal pressures generated by an unsentimental examination of cultural assumptions. The fact that the federal government itself funded experimentation in social science curriculum is not ironic; it is simply symptomatic of our increasing sophistication.

If you detect a heavy charge of pessimism (not to mention uncertainty and ambivalence) running through these remarks you are quite correct. I suppose this is the natural reaction of an evangelist who found that the heathens were surprisingly easy to convert, but dismayingly insistent on being converted on their own terms, which is to say superficially. The capacity of the educational system to accommodate reform and reformers — to swallow them whole without the least sign of indigestion — is awesome and depressing. But, while the schools do seem incorrigibly immune to directed reform they are nonetheless changing. It is probably best to think of planned change as simply one small element in the ecology of education, an element that makes some difference but that cannot really control events.

Jan L. Tucker

Comments on

THE SOCIAL STUDIES,
THE EDUCATIONAL CULTURE,
THE STATE

Can a nation survive if its young people are well educated? This is a genuinely new question in social studies education. And it contains both the hope and the despair of social studies educators. We find in it elements of a Greek tragedy being acted out on the twentieth-century American educational stage. Part of that tragedy is that a teacher who dared raise such a question in his class would probably be given his walking papers. The other part of the tragedy is that unless teachers are given freedom to explore such issues, twentieth-century man may not survive the nation-state. Indeed, to use Mike Scriven's terms, these are issues of "education for survival."

I, too, like Bob, am confused and ambivalent. But I am not pessimistic. In fact, his expression of pessimism gives me hope for the future of social studies education. This hope stems from his candid willingness to question some of his own assumptions — a mark of scholarly self-criticism and integrity which is often lacking in the social studies discourse.

The social studies profession desperately needs to disengage itself from the unproductive arguments centering on the merits of the "new" social studies versus the "old" social studies. We need new arenas and new questions. As Bob has suggested, we need to give at least some attention to the consequences of the possible success of the "new" social studies, the consequences of "social science for all."

The untangling of this complex problem is an uncomfortable burden for the social studies. More of this in a moment. First, I would like to raise several questions about specific points in the paper.

First, Bob has mentioned, and justly so, the stultifying culture of the schools. However, his discussion is dangerously superficial.

For example, more could have been said in a positive fashion about the efforts of the courageous few *within* the schools who are trying to change things. To overlook this point may have the effect of alienating these teachers and administrators who are currently trying to bring about change in the face of very difficult and sometimes threatening circumstances. These people need our help and encouragement, not debilitating stereotyping.

Second, Bob has mentioned that several of the new programs now on the market are doing *very well*. I don't know what this means. Are they selling well? Are they bringing about changed behavior in teachers, schools, and students? And even more obliquely, why won't the "more strictly social science projects" do as well?

And finally, why label your new course history rather than anthropology? This is perhaps merely an innocuous semantical game. However, I suspect a hidden agenda here.

Now allow me to push on by sketching several lines along which the main inquiry which Bob has initiated might develop. This involves questions about the following points: (1) the impact of social science instruction upon elementary and secondary school students; (2) the role of the social science teacher; (3) the consideration of new educational environments for social studies education; and (4) the consequent responsibilities of the developmental projects and teacher education institutions.

The impact of social science instruction upon students. How will the acquisition of social science knowledge affect the behavior patterns of the students? Will this knowledge create understanding, empathy, responsibility, and community, or will it, on the other hand, alienate, discourage, and isolate? Will the teaching of dispassionate social science permit the legitimate voicing of expressive and emotional behaviors? To what extent can our students stand outside their culture and institutions for purposes of social science analysis and remain, on the other hand, a functioning part of that culture? Can we, to borrow an insight from Kenneth Boulding, encourage our students to view Fourth of July celebrations as "tribal rites" and still expect them to participate in the culture that promotes such celebrations?

Unrest in universities and secondary schools can, at least in part, be attributed to the students' realization that fault lines exist between the American dream and American reality. Ought we to promote some conciliatory movement along this fault line in order to relieve the tension, knowing that, in fact, we might be triggering a social earthquake? The point is that we know very little about the behavioral consequences of the acquisition of social science knowledge. And until we get this information it is exceedingly difficult to determine what ought to be the role of the social sciences in general education. These are questions to which social science investigation can provide some answers. And it is my hope that the projects can begin to take on some of these long-range tasks in the next round of social studies curriculum development.

The role of the social science teacher. I have intentionally made no attempt to separate the development of curriculum (defined as content) and the teaching of that curriculum. For purposes of analysis, these functions can be separated. But I think it is unwise, at least in the social studies, for developers to give exclusive attention to one or the other. This reasoning stems from what I believe to be a misleading hope expressed by some of the project directors that the social sciences can be taught successfully by any teacher, so long as the package is programmed correctly and so long as the teacher religiously adheres to this program. I would grant that according to an evaluation scheme based upon the acquisition of knowledge, this hope can very well become a reality. The Sociological Resources for the Social Studies Project — and now Bob tells us it is true of the Anthropology Project as well — has some evidence supporting the ironic generalization that the less academic training for the teacher, the better the students' achievement. However, this whole argument, be it true or false, misses a basic point.

If it is true that social science knowledge has a bearing on how students act in relation to one another and in relation to their institutions, then it is short-sighted in the extreme for the projects to be concerned *only* with producing materials and plugging teacher-technicians into these materials. We should also be interested in additional qualities of the teachers who will be using these materials. I submit that the teaching style of a given teacher which may make him a whiz at implementing the social science "package" may also be the style which tends to make him oblivious to the normative implications of teaching this knowledge. It may be that the teacher who is most comfortable fitting into a programmed curriculum is also the one who is the last to suspect that there may be an intimate relationship between what goes on in his own social science classroom and student behavior, either in that classroom or outside of it. Placing the new social science curricula in the hands of technically competent but normatively blind teachers may be a mistake that we cannot afford. This is one interpretation of Lee Cronbach's distinction between the notion of a well-*trained* teacher and a well-*educated* teacher.

My examples have been intentionally overdrawn in order to emphasize that the materials producers need to take a closer look at the appropriate role of social science teachers. It could be, as I pointed out, that the ability to follow the project-developed teachers' guide is not the most important role attribute. In fact, it may be dysfunctional, given the possibility that students may choose to act unpredictably and in unexpected ways after acquiring this knowledge. This brings me to my third point.

Consideration of new educational environments. I am assuming that social studies educators would like to see student energies and concerns which arise from a teaching of social science channelled into constructive and productive action. It is simply irresponsible and perhaps even impossible to teach social science knowledge without providing students a chance to test this knowledge by either bringing the open society into the schools or taking the school into the open society. We simply are not seriously addressing this point at the present time. The question is not whether we, as educators, shall be responsible for the political actions of students which may be stimulated by social science knowledge. Rather, the question is, given this responsibility, how shall we handle it?

Thus, social studies educators, as Bob has suggested, cannot talk of social science curriculum development apart from important changes in the institutional structure itself. I simply don't believe that elementary and secondary teachers can cope with this problem by themselves. The role conflict is extremely intense and the pressures are overwhelming.

Therefore, my final point is that *both the social studies projects and teacher training institutions need to begin assuming a more direct role in helping the schools to effect and consolidate these*

institutional changes. Among other things, we need to seek ways
to legitimatize the school's function in teaching, learning, and acting upon social science knowledge. The idea of "social science
for all" may well require new types of educational environments,
contrasting markedly with the traditional classroom. If you answer
that this effort is not our responsibility, then I must ask what is
the purpose in teaching the social sciences? What then are some
of the things that we can do to begin building such a legitimacy?

We can begin at the university level, as I noted earlier, by
addressing ourselves to the inconsistencies between what, on the
one hand, we urge that elementary and secondary school teachers
do, and, on the other hand, what we do ourselves. For, in fact,
project directors and social studies educators are generally not
good models of self-criticism and intellectual abrasiveness. And
perhaps more importantly, we can demonstrate by our own actions
the political and moral relationships between our knowledge of
the social sciences and the problems of society which press upon
us. Finally, we can begin to provide leadership in the promotion
of academic freedom for students and teachers with respect to
social science education in general education. Much has been said
about school support systems at this conference. I consider matters
of academic freedom to be at the top of the priority list in the
social studies. Perhaps the most we can say about our efforts in
this area at the present time is that there has been a long, long
silence. It is interesting that non-educational organizations such
as the American Civil Liberties Union have done more in this
regard than we have in education.

In summary, what I have been saying is that the proponents
of the new social studies must begin to nourish, by research and
action, by concept and precept, the kinds of educational environments which will be necessary if the social sciences are going to
become a viable part of social studies instruction. This is one
way of working our way out of the dilemma that Bob has posed.
Let us hope that the nation-state and social science education
can live together in a state of "creative tension." Let us hope
they are not mutually destructive. However, if the proposed
"Guidelines for Moral Instruction" for the California public
schools, reported this very morning in the San Francisco *Chronicle,*
are indicative of the prevailing climate of opinion, the road ahead
will not be an easy one. These "Guidelines" are an excellent

illustration of the basic tension which Bob has identified. As a fitting closing comment permit me to quote the *Chronicle's* report:

TEACHING MORALITY — NAVY STYLE

Los Angeles

A massive set of guidelines for moral instruction in California's public schools that attacks the U.S. Supreme Court, the United Nations and mental health programs was presented here yesterday to the State Board of Education.

If adopted today the 81-page document would become an integral of the Family Life and Sex Education programs in all California public schools.

The guidelines urged school administrators and teachers to pattern their moral training after "the moral leadership program" of the Navy and Marine Corps.

Behavior. The document specifically attempts to "identify that kind of behavior and activity alien to our heritage and/or unlawful and contrary to public policy."

In doing so, it attacks the United Nations, recent rulings of the U.S. Supreme Court, mental health programs in school, sex education, sensitivity training, public acceptance of homosexuality and "the creeping cult of secular humanism." It compared humanists to Communists.

It strikes out at Margaret Mead, John Dewey, Ashley Montague, and psychiatrists who attempt to eradicate guilt and fear in children caused by their concepts of sin or morality.

Heavy emphasis in the reports is placed on God, the Bible, J. Edgar Hoover, George Washington, Thomas Jefferson, Abraham Lincoln, William Buckley Jr. and 100-year-old textbooks.

The guidelines were developed on orders of the State Board of Education Code which says morality will be taught to California school children.

The consensus of the nine-member advisory committee, appointed by State Superintendent Max Rafferty, which drafted the report, is that "a moral crisis is sweeping the land and all aspects of American behavior are affected.

"This moral crisis is reflected in the increased use of drugs at colleges as well as of sexual promiscuity, of illegitimate births, and incredible increases in crimes of violence, especially among teen-agers.

"The staff feels they have developed the proper yardstick by which to measure the valid and invalid, the moral and the immoral, the alien and the unalienable."

The committee was headed by Edwin S. Klotz, who, until last week was Rafferty's liaison between the Department of Education and the State Board of Education.

Removal. Klotz was removed from that post after the Board demanded it because he had been giving speeches around the State advocating right-wing ideas that conflicted with State Board policy.

The committee included three conservative Republican legislators — Assemblymen E. Richard Barnes of San Diego and Floyd Wakefield of Downey and State Senator John L. Harmer of Glendale.

Another member is the Rev. Robert Williams, pastor of the little known Church of Reflection which is located on Knott's Berry Farm in Orange county. Walter Knott, the owner, is a heavy financial contributor to right-wing causes.

The guidelines are based primarily on the Bible and the Ten Commandments, which are spelled out with corresponding Pearl Code sections. The guidelines are built around "Natural Law and Divine Law," and say that "the moral laws which govern mankind remain constant, whatever the political or economic changes in social structure . . ."

With this in mind, the report quotes at length from a textbook used 100 years ago called "Cowdery's Moral Lessons," which contained 30 lessons on manners and morals, "each lesson having a maxim which is illustrated by stories or anecdotes."

Listed are some of the maxims, including "be slow to promise but be sure to perform," "speak evil of no one," "swear not at all," and "be neat."

Stories. The report also referred to the "Willson's Readers," which spoke of "Lazy Slokins, the school boy — drunkard — the thief" and contained other stories called "My Mother's Bible" and "The Beginning of Sin."

Conceding such literature might be "a little harsh and puritanical to our generation," the report nevertheless says such instruction should be reinstituted in the schools.

The guidelines depict the biggest threat to children's morality as the "humanist movement" and called humanism "a 20th century synonym for athiesm."

Warning that humanism is "entrenched in high places," the

report charges the humanists have "created an intellectual confrontation within the educational system which must be recognized," and names Dewey as the "high priest of progressive education."

The guidelines also warn of another "technique of undermining our heritage," "the prevalence of teachers and scholars . . . who concentrate on American failings rather than on American achievements."

The report stated that although it could not "describe the extent of this penetration," the trend needs reversing.[1]

---

[1] Ron Moskowitz, "Teaching Morality — Navy Style," San Francisco *Chronicle*, May 9, 1969, p. 1. © Chronicle Publishing Co., 1969. Reprinted with permission.

SEVEN

ELLIOT W. EISNER

PERSISTENT DILEMMAS
IN CURRICULUM
DECISION-MAKING

The persistent dilemmas of curriculum decision-making about which I would like to speak are not new to the field of education. Like most of the persistent problems in the field, they have been with us for years. Now, however, during a time of social and educational crisis these dilemmas have taken on a saliency that they have seldom had. In this paper, I would like to identify some of these persistent dilemmas and, in so doing, I will be baring my soul concerning some of the problems in curriculum which nag me and for which I have yet to find satisfying solutions. Perhaps this group can suggest ways in which these dilemmas might be resolved. Perhaps the larger question is whether or not the issues that I raise are the ones that are worth raising in the first place.

Let me start with what must be obvious to all of us here: there is emerging in this country a social and educational revolution that is recasting the goals and function of schooling, not only at levels of higher education, but at the secondary and elementary levels as well. This revolution, while having its initial impetus in the black community, is now a movement consisting of the children of the well-heeled, of conscience-ridden liberals, and of varying racial groups, whose chroma range almost throughout the spectrum. What I see as I examine and reflect upon events not only on this campus, but in the high schools around Stanford and in the colleges of the nation is the emergence of a passionately committed mix of disenfranchised minority-group students and intellectual liberal-radicals who like neither what they see in the nation, nor what they have in the schools. I see individuals who once had docile or obsequious relationships with their teachers attempting to redefine their teachers' roles, recasting their roles as students, and redefining the mission of the school. The student groups are concerned not only about the military posture of the country, they are disenchanted with an educational program that they believe has little relevance to their lives. They want, and are demanding, a voice in the curriculum. They want to decide what they shall study and how.[1]

Now the educational goal of enabling students to define their own learning tasks and to establish their own educational aims has been a long-standing ideal among American educators. To prepare students to assume responsibility for their own education, to plan their own educational program, is after all, what most of us in this room, I believe, are interested in as long-range, if not immediate consequences of schooling. The student activist in today's schools wants at the least a partnership in the process of curriculum decision-making. Many of them are objecting to content which strikes them as irrelevant to their immediate concerns, irrelevant to the proper concerns of society, and irrelevant to the type of life that they believe to be worth living.

These concerns with the relevance of curriculum content are not limited to vocal students. The recent moves to decentralize the control of large city school systems is another manifestation of the same concerns. In New York, for example, the legislature has recently passed a law which will divide New York City into thirty to thirty-three school districts, each having its own board of education and administrative organization. Black and Puerto Rican citizens are demanding more than the token influence emanating from the local PTA. They want not only to obtain curriculum relevance for their children, they want to guarantee such relevance by selecting both the principals and teachers who are to work with their children. From their point of view the instructional methods that have been used in the schools, the curriculum that has been provided, indeed the pervasive attitude of the school as a social institution, have failed to facilitate the type of personal development and social mobility that parents demanding decentralized schooling are insisting upon. Some parents believe that the schools have not only failed to facilitate personal growth, but have actually militated against such growth. In their eyes, the school — and especially the program of the school, the curriculum — has created a pathogenic cycle whose rate and severity increase with each passing school day.

Although it is unfortunate that disenchantment with the schools has initiated the demands for control of the curriculum, the goal of enabling students to formulate their own educational purposes has been and continues to be an aim that is prized among educators. We want, I assume, to prepare students who will become increasingly responsible for conducting their own education.

The problem that nags me as I reflect upon this orientation to curriculum decision-making deals with the problem of reconciling it with the ideal of utilizing the best and widest array of knowledge available for deciding upon the content of school programs. On the one hand, we want students to assume responsibility for their own educational program. They won't be in school forever. On the other hand, we want to be able to use large-scale analyses of socio-economic trends, we want to use the data developed by social forecasters, we want to employ theories of cognitive development and learning to guide us in establishing parameters for the content and aims of the curriculum.[2] The forty-three million children and youths who attend American schools are entitled to encounter educational programs that result from the application of the most sophisticated tools that we have available. The content of their programs should develop skills and ideas of enormous power and style, skills and ideas which will endure beyond the ephemeral demands of the present. To create such programs will probably require not less sophistication and insight into the processes of learning, but more sophistication.

How does one provide local communities with the opportunity to decide what shall be taught to their children and, at the same time, draw upon the skills and data of social scientists, curriculum specialists, and educational scholars for building educational programs? One of the tenets of rational curriculum planning calls for the use of a wide variety of specialists and a wide array of data for determining the content and organization of the curriculum. Not only are the characteristics of the students to be considered, but the needs of the society, the demands of the emerging future, and the nature of the fields to be encountered are all believed relevant data for curriculum planning. Curriculum decision-making is seen as one of the most complex aspects of educational planning generally, one which when done well successfully integrates the conclusions provided by a diversified spectrum of specialized personnel. How does such a conception of curriculum development square with the belief that local communities or individual students should assume the primary responsibility for deciding what shall be the object of educational attention?

That the problems of curriculum decision-making are complex and difficult is testified to by the papers and discussions that have taken place in this conference. Are better solutions to be found in more localized curriculum making? Are teachers capable of deciding — even with the aid of students — what is worth attending to educationally? Do we prepare them with such skills? Do teachers have the appropriate array of curriculum options available to them and can they select and cope with the diversity of such options and still assume effective responsibility as teachers? It is clear that one of the assumptions underlying most, if not all, of the national curriculum development projects has been that more educationally significant curricula could be provided in our nation's schools if programs within the various disciplines could be developed by the best minds available. Extensive financial expenditures have been made to bring such people together, to pilot-test and revise prototype programs, and to train teachers to use the new curricula that have been developed. It is estimated that during the past ten-year period the National Science Foundation and the United States Office of Education have made available for curriculum building and in-service teacher education over $100,000,000, all of this in the name of improved educational programs. Can one reconcile curriculum development on a large-scale national basis in which teachers adopt programs developed hundreds of miles from their classrooms with demands to localize — indeed personalize — programs for individual students? Can curriculum decision-making operate both ways? Are there ways of reconciling these apparently opposing approaches to the problems of curriculum development, each of which appears to me to have important virtues? The former approach has the virtue of bringing to the classroom teacher a set of curriculum materials engineered by specialists who purportedly have a depth of understanding in their field of study, material which presents the central and most enduring aspects of that field to the student's attention. The latter approach capitalizes on the student's initiative and demands that teachers, working closely within community policy, develop programs that speak to the particular interests and needs of students in a particular social context. The ramifications of these views have profound consequences for teacher education and curriculum evaluation. These ramifications must, I am sure, be apparent. There is one aspect of the dilemma which lends it even greater complexity.

We know from demographic studies that families are moving from one home to another at an increasingly rapid rate. It is estimated, for example, that over half of the families in the country have been living in their present dwellings for less than five years. What does such mobility imply for the dilemma concerning local or national curriculum planning? Does one conclude that because of family mobility it is especially important for educational programs to have sufficient homogeneity that the child can pick up in his new educational locale without major "retooling"? Or does it imply that precisely because of increased family mobility local curriculum decision-making should be emphasized? Thus the first dilemma that I share with you deals with the apparent problem of choosing between two goods: Can the virtures of community control and student-initiated curriculum making be reconciled with the virtues of large-scale curriculum development? Perhaps this group can suggest ways of resolving this problem.

A second dilemma that nags my educational soul deals with the age-old educational question of how to achieve balance in the curriculum. For decades there has been a strong desire among educators, especially at the elementary school level, to provide a curriculum having "balance." While "balance" is not a term having great precision, I generally take it to mean with respect to the school curriculum that children will have access to the major intellectual and artistic disciplines that have historically been a part of our culture. A variety of scholars — Hutchins, Bestor, Koerner, Phenix, and others — argue that the major fields of inquiry constitute a fundamental core of intellectual and artistic subject matter and that becoming educated requires an understanding and appreciation of the ideas and methods which these fields provide.[3] Phenix has argued that the way man secures meaning from experience is by interpreting his sensations within the frames of reference, or, as Phenix calls them, the realms of meaning, that constitute the disciplines. It then follows that the school curriculum, if it is to provide for the development of educated men, should introduce students to the major realms of meaning and should enable them to use the ideas and modes of inquiry that constitute these realms.

Now the ideal of providing an educational program that will prepare students to derive meaning from experience through the diverse windows that the various arts and sciences provide is surely appealing. In a way, our schools have attempted to achieve this ideal by offering to elementary, and to some degree to secondary and college students, a range of fields and then requiring that students study them. When school curricula became heavily laden with the sciences, both educators and parents became concerned that the ideal of curriculum balance was being sacrificed and that educational redress be provided. In some ways the currently emerging interest in the arts and humanities is evidence of the recognition that the school curriculum has been skewed to the sciences and to mathematics and needs, therefore, to be brought back into balance.[4] Balance in the curriculum has been and is an idealized criterion for deciding upon curriculum content. Like the well-balanced diet, the well-balanced curriculum contributes to educational health.

Yet the goal of balance in curriculum is not without a lusty competitor. While schoolmen are concerned with balance, they also are concerned with, as Harold Benjamin called it, the cultivation of idiosyncrasy.[5] How does one ensure the cultivation of idiosyncrasy while, at the same time, requiring students to study the wide range of subject matters that make for educationally balanced men? By the cultivation of idiosyncrasy, I mean providing students with the opportunity to attend deeply and extensively to the pursuit of their own aesthetic and intellectual interests. By the cultivation of idiosyncrasy, I mean not only providing such opportunities but encouraging students to seek them out and to attend to the development of those particular talents and aptitudes that differentiate one man from another. In practical terms, such an approach might mean neglecting some areas of study completely and giving only a passing nod to others, while immersing oneself in the type of artistic or academic work that "turns one on." The committee that developed the new curriculum policy at Stanford has opted for this choice in revamping the Institution's undergraduate program. The authors of *The Study of Education at Stanford* present their rationale in this way:

> Our faculty must be in the places where knowledge is advanced and with this comes a need in our day to specialize intensively so that the frontiers of knowledge can be reached. This demand derives, we believe, not from the so-called "publish or perish" rule of academic success, but from a complex set of motivations to travel the path of discovery. For the most part it is because faculty members are interested in the unknown or the misunderstood that they have come to the University in the first place. The intense specialization that results from this characteristic of the faculty seems to militate against the demand for "general education" in the traditional sense, with its stress on a common body of knowledge and a concomitant insistence upon a highly prescriptive curriculum. "General education" courses turn out to be an unwelcome chore for both faculty and students in a setting where teaching or learning something prescribed by a committee is rightly looked upon as the bottom of the academic barrel. . . . Let the objective of curricular planning be to encourage the faculty member to teach what he likes to teach and the student to learn what seems vital to him — the intellectual history of Europe in the nineteenth century rather than the history of Western Civilization, modern consciousness rather than freshman English, organizational behavior rather than introduction to sociology — and from this common freedom may emerge a form of general education far better suited to the characteristics of the University than to that to which we pay lip service now.[6]

It is clear in which direction the authors of *The Study of Education at Stanford* have moved. Both teachers and students should, in their view, be free to select their own areas of interest for teaching and learning. Is such an orientation to curriculum viable for American secondary schools? The advocates of this conception of curriculum content believe that the problem of securing breadth of understanding can be resolved by getting students to immerse themselves in the areas of study which are particularly interesting to them. Specialization, they hold, is not contrary to the development of broadly based intellectual interests. By understanding a particular field in depth, the student will somehow come to appreciate the wider array of intellectual tools and artistic achievements that constitute man's cultural past and which enable him to secure significant meaning from the present.

At first blush, this position has an undeniable attractiveness. An in-depth understanding of a field of study can have aesthetic as well as merely instrumental consequences. For the specialist, specialized understanding is probably the only "real" way to understand and appreciate the power and elegance of ideas. Yet, I am not convinced by the thesis that specialization breeds general understanding or that it cultivates an appreciation of the variety of ways in which meaning can be secured. I am painfully aware of my own failure to validate the claim that general appreciation emanates from specialized intellectual focus. And frankly, in general, I am not impressed with the level of intellectual catholicity that my specialized colleagues possess. Thus, the second dilemma: If attention to a wide range of problems and fields of study is necessary for the type of personal and intellectual range one wishes to develop in students, how then can one cultivate, in depth, those idiosyncratic interests and aptitudes which almost all students have?

One putative solution to this dilemma that has emerged rather recently deals with the ideal of fostering high-level cognitive processes in students. Some authorities claim that what schools need is the development of curricula that facilitate problem-solving skills, curricula which enable children to exercise those cognitive abilities that will enable them to cope effectively with problems no matter what the source or mode of presentation. The development of general inquiry skills seems to provide the answer for curricula that are now, according to these authorities, subject-bound. But to me this approach also fails to resolve the issue. Problems come in various shapes, sizes, and media. General process development, like contentless form, is something which I, at least, cannot conceive of. The problems and processes involved in painting and in writing poetry, just to take two art forms as examples, are of different orders. If they were not, poets would be painters and vice versa. Generalized process development unrelated to the characteristics and demands of the particular medium of perception and expression do not appear to me to hold promise for resolving the dilemma of curriculum balance. How can we develop educational programs that give students an appreciation of the reach of man's mind and, at the same time, enable him to savor the experience that comes from study in depth of a particular field?

A third dilemma in curriculum decision-making that I would like to share with you deals with the problem of evaluating the educational consequences of the programs we construct or endorse. One view of evaluation insists on the necessity for formulating precise objectives for the curriculum, objectives which unambiguously specify the behavior of students after they have undergone a series of learning experiences.[7] Some writers on curriculum go so far as to suggest a procedure whereby all behaviors are to be identified and evaluated after each unit of instruction.[8] Such a procedure makes the goals of the curriculum precise and provides clear standards against which to appraise the effectiveness of the curriculum that is being employed. Clarity is salutary; it can increase educational responsibility and eliminate much of the fuzziness characteristic of large quantities of educational literature. As long as goals remain diffuse, curriculum makers can escape responsibility for the programs they produce. Clarity, specificity, precision — these are generally thought to be the necessary ingredients of effective curriculum development. In addition, clarity of objectives makes it possible to identify causal relationships between outcomes and treatment. In so doing, it enables one to establish generalizations concerning act and consequence in curriculum, and thus contributes to our understanding of educational processes.

Associated with this conception of the role of objectives in evaluation is the general belief that product evaluation should occur at the end of the instructional sequence. Generally this evaluation occurs at the end of the semester or course of study. The practice of specifying the objectives of the curriculum and evaluating to determine whether they have been attained rests on the assumption that it is important to know where you are going in curriculum, that you determine through evaluation at the end of an instructional sequence whether or not you have arrived there, and that such data provide evidence of the significance or impact of the curriculum. It is implicitly assumed that evidence of terminal behavior has predictive validity for behaviors to be manifested at a later date.

Notwithstanding the recent array of criticism regarding the

limitations of behavioral objectives and the evaluation practices related to such a conception, one can hardly deny the virtue of having at least *some* relatively clear conception of desired outcomes, as well as the virtue of evaluating in light of those conceptions.[9] As curriculum developers we do have, it seems to me, some responsibility for what we do to students through the programs we build. We do have a responsibility to try to find out what the consequences of our programs are.

Yet despite the virtues of having at least some objectives which are clearly held and of evaluating in relation to them, I am nagged by the belief that assessing student behavior at the end of the instructional unit does not really predict how he is likely to behave, or think, or experience outside the classroom. Grades, as symbols of evaluations, are admittedly the best predictors we have of school performance, but I am not convinced that they predict what is intellectually significant outside of school. If we look to the student's out-of-school performance, and if we wait a significant period of time after the course is completed to observe his behavior — for surely we are not merely interested in immediate post-course behavior — we have a hard time associating the causes of his behavior with the effects of the curriculum. Indeed, the longer we wait, the more difficult the association becomes. Thus arises the bind of being interested in achieving significant personal and social consequences through the curriculum and yet finding it more difficult to account for such consequences the more removed the student is from the program in which he studied.

The resolution of this dilemma might be found in more artful and comprehensive approaches to evaluation. I do not have a full-blown resolution to this problem but I would like to conclude my paper by suggesting an approach that might prove profitable.

It seems to me that it might be useful to develop procedures that would secure a wide range of unobtrusive data on student behavior in settings that more closely approximate than schools now do those settings that the student will find when he leaves school.[10] This suggestion means several things for curriculum evaluation. First, it means that the environment of the school must be changed sufficiently so that the types of interests and abilities that are developed through the school can be displayed in it. This demonstration seldom occurs at present because of the type of social and intellectual constraints which schools as social organizations place upon students. Schools might well develop parameters that more closely approximate the type of social reality that students face in out-of-school settings.

Second, data-gathering mechanisms in the form of unobtrusive measures and other types of tracking procedures need to be developed to provide a much more comprehensive picture of where students are in relation to where they have been and to where they appear to be going. These new procedures will require a far greater emphasis on the development of skills of clinical criticism among teachers than we currently emphasize either in the training of teachers or in the area of evaluation.[11] Clinical assessments are somehow considered suspect; they contain "none" of the objectivity that comes from examining the Kuder-Richardson 20. Yet the teacher sees an infinitely wider range of evidence than any achievement test now published provides. Such observation, when refined and critical, needs to hold a greater, not a lesser place in curriculum evaluation.

Third, we will need to learn how to synthesize the data secured from such diverse procedures to create a meaningful evaluation mosaic for both the student and the group. Putting together such data is a synthetic art. It will require an approach and a set of skills that are now absent in the evaluation literature. I do not have, at this time, specific suggestions to make regarding the way this synthesis might be accomplished; I believe that our current approaches to educational evaluation — even some of the new concepts in the field — are far from adequate nets for capturing the educational outcomes of schooling. New modes of evaluation resting upon new assumptions need to be developed. I have tried to suggest one approach.

In this paper, I have attempted to share with you some of the dilemmas that puzzle me as I reflect upon curriculum decision-making. The first dilemma dealt with the virtues of local control of curriculum versus the virtues of large-scale curriculum planning. The second dealt with the problem of curriculum balance. The third dealt with the relationship between clarity in short-term evaluation and the possibility of developing more comprehensive and richer, although perhaps less objective evaluations of the student's development. The problems these dilemmas pose are, for me, difficult ones. I wish I had some neat answers. I do not. Perhaps the discussion and the respondent's comments will lighten my load. I eagerly await your observations.

REFERENCES

[1] Evidence for this is apparent too often to mention, but groups such as the SDS and neighborhood communities, espicially in black ghettos, are typical sources of disenchantment with standard forms of curriculum decision-making.

[2] Perhaps the classic statement in the use of diversified personnel in determining the content and aims of the curriculum is to be found in Franklin Bobbitt's *How to Make a Curriculum,* New York: Houghton Mifflin Co., 1924.

[3] Robert Maynard Hutchins, *The Conflicts in Education in a Democratic Society,* New York: Harper, 1953; Arthur Bestor, *Educational Wastelands; the Retreat from Learning in Our Public Schools,* Urbana: University of Illinois Press, 1953; James D. Koerner, *The Case for Basic Education,* Boston: Little, Brown and Co., 1959; Phillip Phenix, *Realms of Meaning; A Philosophy of the Curriculum for General Education,* New York: McGraw-Hill, 1964

[4] For an example of the curriculum theorists concern for balance see *Balance in the Curriculum,* ASCD Yearbook, 1961.

[5] Harold Benjamin, *The Cultivation of Idiosyncrasy,* Cambridge: Harvard University Press, 1949.

[6] *The Study of Education at Stanford: Report to the University,* Stanford: Stanford University Press, 1968.

[7] See for example Robert Mager. *Preparing Educational Objectives for Programmed Instruction,* San Francisco: Feron Publishers, 1961.

[8] Robert Gagné, "Curriculum Research and the Promotion of Learning," *AERA Monograph Series on Education,* No. 1, Chicago: Rand McNally & Co., 1968.

[9] For a distinction between types of objectives and the relationship of evaluation to them, see E. W. Eisner, "Instructional and Expressive Objectives: Their Formulation and Use in Curriculum," *Instructional Objectives,* Monograph No. 3, Washington: American Educational Research Association, 1969.

[10] An approach to the type of measures that might prove useful are found in Eugene J. Webb, *et al., Unobtrusive Measures,* Chicago: Rand McNally, 1966.

[11] Clinical criticism is a new term in educational discourse. It implies the use of both clinical psychological methods and the methods of art criticism. Its end is to illuminate phenomenon and then correct what is faulty or impaired.

Merlin C. Wittrock

Comments on

PERSISTENT DILEMMAS
IN CURRICULUM DECISION-MAKING

In his excellent and stimulating talk, Elliot Eisner discussed three important dilemmas in curriculum building. The theme of his talk, which is implicit in these dilemmas, is concern for the individual learner. Elliot and I share this concern very much. Apparently we both believe that when we discuss curricula and curriculum building we need to think about individual learners and their reaction to the curricula.

Using his theme, concern for the individual, I want to respond to his paper and to the three dilemmas raised there. The basis of my response is that we have information and conceptualizations about learners and about human learning. These conceptualizations introduce concern for the individual and give us bases for approaching the complex issues he introduced.

With Elliot, I see no simple solutions to these three dilemmas. However there are ways to make progress toward their resolution. One way is for curriculum builders and educational psychologists to work together, using their knowledge about curriculum and human beings to improve student learning, our understanding of learners, and the process of constructing curricula.

The approach I am using to respond to Elliot's paper will, I hope, lead our discussions and thinking to focus upon producing useful generalizations about curriculum building. By combining knowledge of subject matter and curriculum building with information about learners and the process of learning, perhaps we can further develop our understanding of curriculum building.

Adapting to individual differences. Let us begin by briefly reviewing each of the three dilemmas Elliot discussed. I will then turn to a conceptualization of learning already introduced and discussed at this conference and attempt to relate the two — the dilemmas and the conceptualization — to each other.

The first dilemma raised by Elliot dealt with local and individual control of curriculum design versus large-project control of curricula. In his words: "Can the virtues of community control and student-initiated curriculum making be reconciled with the virtues of large-scale curriculum development?" This first issue involves the social and educational rebellion we find on our campuses today, the students' desires to determine educational goals and curricula in terms of their own interests and felt needs, and the advantages of having curriculum specialists design and construct curricula for use nationally.

The second dilemma Elliot mentioned dealt with balance in the curriculum. He talked about balance in several different ways: balance in terms of breadth versus depth, balance in terms of an emphasis on science versus an emphasis on art, and balance also in terms of individuality and idiosyncrasies. Here again, the essential theme of his paper, concern for the individual, is seen in the statement of his second dilemma: "How can we develop educational programs that give students an appreciation for the reach of man's mind and, at the same time, enable him to savor the experience that comes from study in depth of a particular field?"

The third dilemma dealt with something that has been close to my heart for the last several years — evaluation. Elliot raised this issue with respect to short-term, clearly stated objectives and procedures for evaluation versus a more comprehensive, sophisticated evaluation emphasizing the transfer of effects of curricula to students' lives outside of school.

I felt strongly enough about this issue to start a Center on Evaluation at UCLA, and I used this same theme to write the proposal for the Center. With Elliot, I believe that in evaluation we need comprehensive, sophisticated approaches emphasizing transfer of learning.

These three dilemmas are significant issues that concern all of us. As I stated before, one way to make progress toward their solution is to try to apply to them knowledge from educational psychology — conceptualizations of learning, instruction, and curriculum decision-making — that will introduce added concern for the individual learner.

Let us begin with a conceptualization of learning. Ben Bloom has presented this conference with a model of learning called learning for mastery. He said that these kinds of conceptualizations are not used as frequently as they should be to help us make decisions about curricula. I agree with him.

Let us see what might happen if we take seriously the concept of learning for mastery, and apply it to the three dilemmas that Elliot raised a few moments ago. We could use other approaches, such as the model Macdonald discussed briefly at this conference. But Ben's model is a good choice. It has already been presented to you in some detail. If time permits I will also mention implications from Lee Cronbach's approach to studying interactions between treatments and individual differences in aptitudes.

Let us start with the first dilemma introduced by Elliot, local versus national control of curriculum building. If I follow Ben's model, the survival skills could be quite well taught, the materials prepared, and the goals determined nationally without student involvement in the making of decisions about these activities. These activities might also be performed with some student involvement, but at least with the teaching of the survival skills it seems clear that we would have professionals and teachers agreeing upon goals and constructing the curricula. We might have one set of materials used with a wide variety of students, or at least one set of goals applied to nearly all students.

His model would allow a great deal of individualization of instruction in terms other than the goals. These would include the possibility of having as many different methods of instruction as we have students. There would be different rates of presentations and different sequences of instruction. This approach makes sense with the teaching of survival skills, provided society and its emissaries are in agreement about what the skills of survival are.

Concerning the issue of balance in the curriculum, we would have considerable freedom to select among subjects not dealing with survival skills. Goals in these areas could also vary according to student interests or according to local and community interests.

Last of all, if I follow Ben's model, the evaluation of curriculum is to be determined by the crucial nature of the survival skills to be taught. To me this statement implies content validity and careful measurement of the crucial skills acquired by the students. I read into his model a comprehensive approach towards evaluation, including transfer. It would not be sufficient to ensure survival of a society for a student simply to demonstrate learning in a school situation. His behavior would have to transfer outside the school. In sum, I see applications to each of Elliot's three dilemmas deriving from Ben's model of learning for mastery.

Let me take a moment to mention another approach to learning and instruction. Lee Cronbach has studied and written about individual differences in aptitude interacting with treatments in instruction. His approach also has implications for the problems just discussed. In some ways, Lee's and Ben's approaches are compatible with each other. One possible difference between their approaches is that Lee emphasizes an open system with different goals for different students. At least this is the position presented in his chapter in Gagné's book *Learning and Individual Differences*.

In his chapter, Lee suggests that one can change instructional procedures and also change goals of learning to accommodate individual differences. He points out that we have been doing this. We have college preparatory curricula for some students and vocational curricula for others. We do change goals for different students. Several other implications could also be taken from his approach but we have time to mention only one of them. He discusses transfer, and he would also obtain measures of transfer to situations outside the classroom.

These two models do not solve our problems of curriculum design, but they do provide bases from which to begin to make progress. They give us some consistency, something to rely on when new problems are raised, so that we need not approach each problem in curriculum as if it were completely new and unique. If we are consistent with an approach, we have some basis to deal sensibly with a variety of problems.

By referring to Bloom's and Cronbach's approaches, I do not mean to be arguing for these two models in particular. Instead I am arguing for a strategy of trying to conceptualize important problems in a way that cuts across different curriculum projects and different fields to the most useful extent possible, and builds upon what is known about individual differences, learning, and instruction to make decisions about curriculum building.

The next step beyond applying the kinds of models that I have discussed involves creating others which use knowledge from the subject-matter disciplines. I hope this conference will cause us to think about developing models that go beyond psychology, evaluation, or education to include knowledge about subject matter.

As I see it, the dilemmas raised by Elliot are issues involving models and empirical research concerning the adaptation of instruction to individual differences. Using conceptions of learning and instruction is one way, I feel, by which we can make progress toward understanding the important issues Elliot discussed in his paper. Bloom's and Cronbach's approaches do not and cannot save us from difficult decisions about curricula, but their approaches or others like them provide the basis and the consistency from which to begin work on these questions, to relate these questions to each other, and to proceed sensibly to make decisions about curricula.

As a next step we need to look further into the issues of when students can logically participate in the choice of goals and sequences of instruction, which individual differences are crucially relevant to curricula, and how we can design a multi-variate evaluation of the outcomes of instruction. The basic issue is how and under what conditions do we adapt instruction to individual differences?

Cause-and-effect evaluation. I would like now to mention other ideas of mine about the issues Elliot discusses. First, I think we need a new type of comprehensive approach to evaluation. In curriculum evaluation studies one aim is to establish cause-and-effect relations between learners and instruction on the one hand, and learning on the other hand, so that work with curriculum projects can contribute generalizations to educational research.

The statistical methodology for cause-and-effect evaluation has been developed in econometrics, sociology, and other fields. A book entitled *Evaluation of Instruction,* edited by David Wiley and me, will be published soon. It presents new approaches to evaluation and includes articles which introduce a methodology for obtaining cause-and-effect relations from the data of evaluation studies. With this methodology, I hope, curriculum projects will be better able to contribute to knowledge about education. This contribution could provide an impetus to educational research.

Transfer of learning. Before reaching my last point, I want to talk briefly about the question of transfer of learning, a question to which I have devoted years of research. Most of my research has been aimed at trying to produce and to measure transfer, to get at the problem involved in the question: Is teaching in any way affecting behavior outside of school?

There are ways of measuring some types of transfer. For example, suppose we are trying to measure transfer after teaching a six-year-old child about condensation. After the instruction was finished we could present him a glass of ice water with moisture condensed on the outside of the glass. We could ask him where the condensation came from. If this is a problem he has not previously seen in school, clearly transfer from his school learning to a common situation is involved. I have found that item to be useful for measuring whether or not a child understands condensation, evaporation, and the concept of molecules. When a child can give a meaningful explanation of how the molecules of water vapor in the atmosphere condensed on the outside of a glass, we probably have evidence that there is learning occurring in the curriculum.

Transfer is a crucial measure to obtain in evaluation studies. It is a long-neglected area in educational research, but it has use and relevance for people working in curriculum projects. Unfortunately, I do not have time to talk about measuring other types of transfer, but it is a problem that should receive more of our energy and resources.

Student dilemmas. The last point I would like to make is that I was pleased by Elliot's paper because it raises issues important not only to me but to my students, both undergraduates and graduates. Let me tell you a story to make that point. Last Monday, shortly before noon, Elliot's paper arrived in the mail. My office is located on the UCLA campus directly over Meyerhoff Park, a little area of the campus reserved for students. It is complete with podium, microphone, and loudspeakers. Students are free to use this area during lunch hour. I have interesting lunch hours. For the last several years I have eaten lunch to the background music of drums and electric guitars, followed with talks by student activists about "relevant" issues, such as the meaninglessness of some curricula, ROTC, sex, pot, and Mayor Yorty. Last Monday, with the usual background music and speeches during the noon hour, I read Elliot's paper.

If he were still alive, Ivan Pavlov would be delighted to know that I now associate the background music and the speeches with the issues and the dilemmas raised in Elliot's paper. As a result, when I again read the paper last night, I found myself hearing guitars and hearing words about relevance and meaning. A conditioned urgency came through to me. His issues were "relevant."

I hope that when you think of his issues you will also think of the students' dilemmas and the students' issues. It is time for us to formulate constructive ideas about how, when, and under what conditions students should be involved in selecting their own curricula, their own instructional devices and procedures and, indeed, their own goals. We need to think also about the conditions under which students definitely should not be involved in these issues. They have ideas, but they need conceptualizations.

It would be very unfortunate if we were not to provide leadership to them at this time. We can begin in small ways. When a student asks us, "Is my education relevant?" we might lead him to examine his concept of relevance — relevant to what? We might retort with, "Is your relevance educational?" I do not mean to be cryptic or to play upon words. I mean that not everything that a student considers to be "relevant" has educational value.

We can also point out that sometimes disciplines seem to be irrelevant because much is known about them or because we don't bother to analyze the problem to see its basic dimensions. Social problems may not seem to involve disciplines, such as mathematics, simply because we either know how to do the math involved in them or we don't understand the relationship between mathematics and the problems. In either case mathematics may seem irrelevant. If we were to stop teaching mathematics for a generation, it would become sizzlingly relevant to the social problems. I do not know how to make this point to some students but I will continue to try.

But I do know that when I return to my office next Monday I will hear the familiar music and the speeches with the familiar arguments. And in good Pavlovian tradition, I will think of Elliot's paper and his three dilemmas.

Although we do not have answers to these dilemmas, we do have conceptualizations, ideas, and empirical research findings "relevant" to them. Let us not make the mistake of ignoring what we have learned, of considering it to be irrelevant. We have information and concepts about people, about individuality, about learning, and about instruction. I urge curriculum specialists and educational psychologists to work together, to use our knowledge and our minds to try to solve these three dilemmas. We have "relevant" research and concepts. Let's use them.

PART TWO

REFLECTIONS ON
THE CONFERENCE

EIGHT

EDMUND BURKE FELDMAN

THE NON-VERBAL FIELDS
AS NEGLECTED AREAS
OF STUDY

By "non-verbal fields" I mean those activities and modes of study usually designated "art," "music," "drama," and "dance." A consensus appears to be developing as to a comprehensive term for their role in school curricula — aesthetic education. This term is preferable to "non-verbal" because verbal language is a very necessary part of teaching in these as in other areas. But the objects that are made or studied in a program of aesthetic education appeal characteristically through their qualities of sight, sound, movement, or their combinations. The logic and grammar of words is usually a minor or nonexistent feature of their form. Still, schooling is conducted as if verbal language were the only means available to children and adolescents for dealing meaningfully with their environment. Why is this so?

We know full well that children learn a great deal through seeing, for example. But we do not know a great deal about how to organize their visual learning systematically, i.e., under the auspices of schools. Even if classrooms were turned into theatres, museums, or concert halls, we would have some difficulty in organizing purposefully what children see, hear, and make there, and we would have even greater difficulty in evaluating what they have learned. That is because our most highly developed tools for structuring teaching effort and measuring its results are verbal or quasi-verbal.

McLuhan notwithstanding, the development of verbal languages in high civilizations precludes the possibility that they will be supplanted by some non-verbal language devoted mainly to the affectivities or the emotions. The practical problem confronting curriculum makers, therefore, is to devise means of gaining access to non-verbal learning through the verbal languages we write and speak. This is not an insurmountable problem when we consider that many of our transactions with the environment entail behaving verbally after engaging in some type of non-verbal activity. In other words, it is very natural to *say* something after you have *seen* or *felt* something. What we say in such transactions often exhibits some of the rudimentary forms of art criticism. What I call art criticism is something everyone does, once it is assumed that (1) everything in the man-made environment is art, (2) any kind of talk about art constitutes some type of art criticism, and (3) some people are more skilled at art criticism than others.

According to the argument above, aesthetic education (the study of non-verbal expression) focuses ultimately on the development of critical skills with respect to organized visual, dramatic, and musical forms. As soon as we mention the term *art criticism,* however, we imply verbal language — discourse. We also become engaged in the problem of guiding student perceptions of organized art objects and presiding over the process of translating these perceptions into publically visible forms — forms that can be spread out discursively and examined in the light of our educational objectives. In other words, we create the possibility of establishing curricula for aesthetic education, we can perceive the goals implicit in such curricula, and we can devise verbal instruments for assessing the effectiveness of teaching in arriving at these goals.

NINE

JAN L. TUCKER

CHALLENGES TO THE "COMMON SCHOOL": IMPLICATIONS FOR CURRICULUM

Item: Black community leaders establish Nairobi High School, a private school designed to promote black culture. Reason: The public schools cannot accommodate a curriculum designed to promote the values of its black constituency.

Item: Three hundred parents, predominantly middle- and upper-income whites, propose a foundation-supported "community" secondary school for their children. This school would serve as an alternative to the existing publicly supported high schools in this particular community. Reason: The public schools cannot accommodate a curriculum designed to deeply engage the students in important political, aesthetic, social, and economic issues and diverse life styles in the community.

Item: A teacher in training writes, "A final but important aspect of my teaching social studies is the fact that I will be working in a traditional public school. Hopefully, this will be a temporary situation and that in not too many years I will teach in a private school of a very different nature. [Reason:] There are certain characteristics of public schools which I consider reprehensible. The first is the fact that students are coerced into learning and are not allowed to learn and develop naturally. Second is the fact that very little recognition is given to the differences between children and the different pace at which they mature. Third is the emphasis on competition and success which molds individuals to fit passively into the economic and social system and to do what is expected of them."

These are but three examples of a broader development which reflects a shift in public attitudes regarding the support, control, and perhaps ultimately the purpose of American education. For at least a century, the American people have generally supported the "common school" conception of education. This includes the notions that elementary and secondary schooling should be publicly controlled and supported, compulsory, open to all, and should offer a common curriculum in order to ensure a cultural cohesion. To be sure, alternatives to the common school have continued to exist. But this should not obscure the fact that the major educational thrust of the past century has been predicated on the common school, writ continually larger. Radical ideas of one era, however, have a tendency to become the conventional wisdom of the next.

In retrospect, a major omission of this curriculum conference was the failure to address ourselves to the consequences of the increasingly salient fact that the "common school" conception of education is now being seriously challenged. A growing number of people for many different reasons apparently believe that this conception of education is a threat to their values. With several important exceptions, notably the papers given by Macdonald, Hanvey, and Eisner, this conference tacitly accepted the prevailing common school "mentality" as an unexamined first principle and an unalterable given.

It is strange that a group most interested in school curriculum would be the last to heed the importance of the strong signals of social discontent and increasing disenchantment with the common school. But it is also understandable, because the discourse about school curricula has been an integral part of the growth and development of the common school. As professional educators interested in curriculum problems, we have cut our educational teeth on the common school and have diligently promoted its values. Even our vocabulary, to a large extent, reflects our assumption that the large majority of our children will be in common schools and that the function of this schooling is the building of a common culture. Thus we talk of scope, sequence, balance, structure, and common learnings. These curriculum concepts do not make a great deal of sense apart from the homogenizing function of the common school. But the curriculum profession must now confront the probability that important groups which heretofore have actively or passively supported its efforts are now abandoning some of the educational values which have secured this relationship.

The "public" served by the common school has always been multiple and pluralistic. The important difference today is that until recently these "publics," at least those who controlled the schools, cooperated toward a common goal, molding diversity into unity. Today, some important "publics" are withdrawing from the common school arena. To the extent that these newly concerned "publics" value pluralism over "uniformity," and to the degree that the common school cannot adjust to these new demands, to that same extent we can expect to witness an increasing flight from the common schools.

The implications of this trend tend to boggle the professional mind. We are not well equipped to deal with the problem, because it is emotional as well as cognitive. Most of us have been committed to the view that the common school is the cornerstone of education in a democratic society. College and university schools of education have been developed to serve and promote this end. Thus, the challenges to the common school may present a real threat to the values of the very professionals who are being asked to assume new leadership roles.

The curriculum profession is caught on the horns of a dilemma. On the one hand, we value the basic principles of the common school, but we know that we must begin to probe its basic assumptions in the light of changing social values. On the other hand, if we actively promote alternatives, this may further fragment and splinter a profession which has struggled mightily to achieve a modicum of conceptual and professional coherence.

There is no intention here to suggest that the common school will soon be replaced by a variety of alternatives. This institution is deeply engrained in American life. The long-range possibility of change, however, is not beyond the realm of imagination. Just as the common school earlier emerged as a result of preference for uniformity over plurality, the reverse is possible if value priorities are changed. The alternatives are becoming more numerous, more powerful, and most importantly they are assuming increasing democratic legitimacy. Professionals in the field of curriculum are required to be aware of this phenomenon, and conceivably will eventually be forced to make choices between the common school and the many alternatives.

While our choices will be determined in large part by our values, they should also hinge upon empirical understanding. In this vein, we need considerably more information about the groups who are withdrawing from the common schools and those who are choosing to stay. It is conceivable, if the trend continues, that in ten years the common school population will be much more homogeneous than at present, the dissident groups having established their own alternatives. If this change occurs and curriculum professionals are not cognizant of it, we may find ourselves "doing our thing" with a far different kind of common school population than exists presently. At the very least, this eventuality could lull us into a false sense of well-being, because those who chose to stay would not be disposed to criticize our assumptions and our curricula. More importantly, we might find ourselves implicitly supporting and even actively promoting a very invidious social-class stratification.

Related implications include questions about the support of schools. It can be assumed that those who support alternatives to the common school conception will not favor plowing large amounts of their own tax monies into the latter. The one available means whereby supporters of often competing alternatives can voice their mutual opposition to the common schools is to vote down increased school tax levies and bond issues. It is apparent to even the most casual observer of the contemporary educational scene that this is happening with increasing frequency. Here we find a subtle but vitally significant curriculum paradox. Curriculum innovation requires capital outlay. This capital is becoming increasingly scarce at the local level. Thus, curriculum innovators look to the federal government. However, the flight from the common school means that the federally supported curriculum projects may be instituted in schools that have in the meantime lost the very constituencies that might benefit most from the innovations. Moreover, there exists one group which resists the prescriptiveness of the federally supported curriculum projects and views the projects as one more crude attempt to enforce uniformity and stifle diversity. For this group, the national curriculum projects may only reinforce existing discontent, thereby contributing to the flight from the schools.

In summary, this Cubberley Curriculum Conference has failed to adequately address itself to problems entailed in the "challenges to the common school." It has been suggested that such discourse is extremely uncomfortable for the curriculum profession because of its historically close identification with the ideal of the common school. However, it was also pointed out that avoidance of distressing issues is no solution. To avoid them would quite probably remove curriculum discourse from all contact with the changing values evidenced in American education. Moreover, ignoring the "challenges to the common school" may make it impossible for curriculum theorists to influence the de- would quite probably remove curriculum discourse from all confrontation with the issues may split the profession asunder. It is not easy to make a choice between impotence and internecine warfare. Perhaps there are other choices; but in any event it is high time that we initiate some activity which indicates that we are at least aware of the complex issues involved.

TEN

IRVING KAUFMAN

INDIVIDUAL DIFFERENCES AND GENERAL EDUCATION

Each student exists as his own person. As such, he is not merely a particular collection of individual differences which may be abstractly formulated, categorized, and normatively attended to. He is distinctively unique, possessed of his own senses and perceptions, his own memories, cupidities, and needs. It may be said that this individuality transforms experience into knowledge or understanding as attentiveness is animated to vital and concrete conditions. Such characteristically private but real concerns also contain, in an existential sense, what the student will become in the future. This future, which education proposes to shape, may be embodied in a curriculum stressing social goals and intellectual aims as well as personal ends. However, within a critical educational context, the future of any one student must be regarded as of an open and unified nature. A student decides what he actually is to learn. It is the result of personal imaginativeness, commitment, and acceptance of relevance, as well as academic capacity. There is an absorption and an activity prior to any extrinsic theorizing. How the student learns is not only established by the choice he makes among alternatives, but is defined by his particularly expressive manner of making those intuitive and intellectual choices. This is more a free initiative, intrinsically motivated rather than channeled by the ideology of any systematized approach. Learning and understanding, individually felt and valued, are no hypothetical listings of methodological and behavioral patterns. They are the actual resolutions of creative yet contingent educational tensions in singular ways. Exploration, inventiveness, and discovery in the classroom, as elsewhere, derive their energy from a personal intelligence which permits the individual student to both know and create his world.

Of necessity, even formalized teaching must accept the enormous variability of individual responses to the environment of education especially as they are set within the qualitative dimensions of distinct disciplines or in new areas of knowledge and human concern. In accepting such an openness of attitude and respect for the inherent worth but idiosyncratic nature of each student, education also merges means with ends or at least recognizes an organic correspondence between the two — a factor of which curriculum theorists need always to be aware. Means become, not tightly managed patterns of learning, but the unique learning characteristics of an individual examining knowledge or ways of knowing. These characteristics command respect even after the abstractions of learning theories are presented. Ends are established, not as prescriptions, but as the natural functions of knowledge and intuition accepted after examination of the nature and purposes of experience or human actions.

The curriculum, in this sense, would serve each student as a suggestive guide rather than a prescriptive directory of parts. It would be regarded as protecting the uninhibited and personally progressive learning of the student, stimulating further spontaneous and intentional growth in both the intuitive and intellectual realms. Yet, there are processes of socialization and a body of common knowledge which education has accepted as its responsibility to transmit to students. It is around these relatively utilitarian aspects that school curricula have been traditionally structured. Unfortunately, despite lip service to the institutionalized cliché of individual differences, the structuring is girded by a regulating academic propriety and a directed social engineering making for a prescriptive curriculum construction. The current failure of such a pedagogy, whatever its past efficacy, is attested to in the widespread disaffection of students, in the non-learning climate which traduces so many other students, all factors leading to the alarming state of crisis in which education finds itself.

Conceivably, as some theorists now speculate, no one generalized curriculum will meet contemporary needs. There may have to be a variety of alternative curricula which offer differentiated cues: for intuitive as well as for analytical thinking; for open ways of knowing in the arts, sciences, the humanities, and social areas; for disparite student groups and different geographical or social surroundings; for discipline and also child-centered concerns. However, these curricula need to be more than merely expedient reforms, they must be reforms which cater to the individual rather than just to the cliché of individual differences. Perhaps curriculum theorists should divest themselves of academic ideologies once they are aware of them. The ideological nature of prized methodologies has colored curriculum construction with social and cultural conditioning in many instances. For example, the intrinsic dignity and worth of each student existing in the here and now has been ignored in favor of model building which projects students as behavioral machines subject to idealized yet frequently skewed theories.

At some points, formal curriculum structure can be eliminated. There may be learning experiences which glow from an involvement with places — an entire city, a factory, a museum, a store, a theatre, or a studio; there may be learning generated by an I–Thou dialogue with people normally not found in schools — artists of all kinds, scholars, professional workers, even ordinary mothers and fathers; and learning may be predicated upon real life rather than academic situations — artistic endeavors, work-study programs (even for youngsters), community service, and travel. These modifications of educational structure to include more than academic and classroom regimen draw upon personal inclination. They expand a developing interest which finds realization in individual commitment and effort.

Such a change in and loosening of educational opportunities to include "occasional" or "incidental" learning does not discount essentials or slough off curriculum commonalities. It simply recasts their learning in honestly individual and contemporary terms. In fact, an opening up of the range of curriculum possibilities may very well reinforce those areas of intellectual rigor and academic expansiveness for which schools like to believe they provide opportunities. Then, indeed, alternative yet pertinent curricula could be structured for the students in schools, curricula which offer appropriate points of entry for inquiring minds and willing spirits. However, the curriculum maker can succeed in such an undertaking only if he accepts the contingent and suggestive nature of his efforts as they touch upon the genuine individuality out of which each person creates his own world.

ELEVEN

BENJAMIN S. BLOOM

ALTERNATIVE APPROACHES TO THE ORGANIZATION OF CURRICULUM AND INSTRUCTION

Instruction at the secondary level and above is largely departmentalized and restricted to a subject-by-subject organization. This approach reflects a relatively ancient and to some extent outmoded view of the specialization of scholarship and research at the university level. In large part, this approach is dictated by the specialized nature of teacher training which prepares a teacher to teach mathematics, French, history, etc. This approach fits in well with the departmentalization of the schools (a necessary administrative organization as schools are created with ever larger numbers of students and teachers). Finally, the subject organization of instruction is further constricted by the curriculum constructers' and educational material developers' sense of what can be accomplished in the way of consensus, efficiency of effort, and market for their products.

The subject organization of instruction does enable teachers to specialize and to become professionals who are proficient in a restricted body of content and approach to instruction. It promotes the development of professional organizations dedicated to particular subjects in the school. While there are advantages to the subject organization, the most gentle way of putting the matter is that the curricular and departmental organization of instruction is primarily designed for the teacher — not for the students. The problems that the individual encounters in life or society do not fit neatly into the course organization found in the schools.

It is not likely that pleas and admonitions will make for a major shift in this curricular organization. Too many vested interests — teachers, university scholars, curriculum makers, textbook publishers, and even parents — all ally to hold the curriculum and instruction in the present highly segmented organization. Also, some of the strengths of the system, strengths which eventually relate to the professional and scholarly occupations, argue against a precipitous shift in the entire system.

However, one can argue for research and experimentation with alternative organizations. One minor shift is away from the narrow subject-course organization, for example, physical sciences as contrasted with physics, chemistry, geology, etc., or social sciences as contrasted with history, civics, psychology, etc. Such a broad-field organization permits the curriculum to escape from a very narrow and pedantic view of knowledge. The broad-field approach to knowledge and learning permits a variety of related disciplines to enter into the consideration of a problem, be it a view of man or nature, or an approach to inquiry.

Perhaps a major shift is to a more open curriculum approach based on problems, case studies, and encounters with the concerns of modern man. What is urged here is that side by side with the subject-matter curriculum a portion of the school time — pehaps as much as a third of the total — should be devoted to the problems, concerns, and interests of contemporary life. Here is where the school might free students to probe more deeply into the issues of current life, the conflicts, and the problems man is encountering or will encounter in the future. One might hope that students as well as faculty would determine the problems and that both would share in the experience of probing, reading, observing, and searching for resolution. In this approach, the organization of material along the case-method approach might constitute the curriculum maker's task. However, it would remain with students and teachers to go beyond this to the problems, the gathering of observations and information, and the analyses that seem appropriate.

In sum, it is suggested that curriculum, instruction, and learning would be strengthened considerably if two or more alternative ways of viewing knowledge, man, and contemporary life existed side by side. One is devoted to the history of man's storage and retrieval of knowledge; the other is devoted to the life and concerns of contemporary man. One is built on the most academic lines; the other is built on the realities as man encounters them.

It is the view of this curriculum conference that schools, teachers, and curriculum workers should develop and experiment with alternative organizations of the curriculum and instruction and that, where possible, two or more approaches to the curriculum and learning should exist simultaneously.

TWELVE

MERLIN C. WITTROCK

INDIVIDUAL DIFFERENCES AND CURRICULA

Underlying the fundamental issues in curriculum development is the question of how we can build curricula to help different students learn in ways most appropriate for them. Do curriculum materials designed for nation-wide use suffice to teach a given subject to fast and slow, boy and girl, reflective and impulsive, and global and analytic students? Or do we need to design different curriculum materials for different individuals, to build upon their individualities, idiosyncrasies, interests, and previous learning?

We could ask the same question about goals of instruction and methods of teaching. But the central point is to ask this question now. By asking it now that we have nationally used curriculum materials, we will inevitably further the development of refined and differentiated approaches to curriculum building. We need to encourage curriculum builders and people who study individual differences, learning, and teaching to work together and to build curricula together. By working together they can help to resolve student dilemmas about meaningful and relevant curricula, and they can build our understanding of the design and use of curricular materials for individuals.

THIRTEEN

ROBERT G. BRIDGHAM

ON TEACHING . . .
VERSUS TEACHING
ABOUT . . .

In many cases the literature on curricular aims displays or suggests a basic choice between "teaching . . ." and "teaching about. . . ." The choice is implicit in much of the discussion at the Cubberley Conference. It is made in various ways by the developers of the new curricula; but it is rarely seen or discussed as generic in curriculum decisions.

Each of the "subjects" of the curriculum has a counterpart in some valued and nurtured form of human activity. The "worth" of a subject in the curriculum is derived, in large measure, from the value of its counterpart activity. The curriculum represents an attempt to bring students to an understanding of the activity. An activity, however, may be valued for different reasons and in different ways by a practitioner of the activity and by an interested non-practitioner. The activity may be represented by the practitioner's experience or by the onlooker's reaction to the activity and its consequences. The choice of representation is important in the curriculum: Should we "teach . . ." — i.e., provide the experience of a new activity? or should we "teach about . . ." — i.e., consider the import for human existence of the activity and its products? The curriculum developed will be strongly affected by the choice.

Advocates of "teaching . . ." stress the priority of the practitioner's experience, and the importance of the *activity* in human affairs. The aim of the curriculum is to bring the student to inquire, as does the scientist; to write, as does the journalist or essayist; to create, as does the painter; to reason, as does the mathematician or philosopher. Students are to be active; the curriculum aims at the improvement of their activity. The improvement of an activity is assessed by comparing it with the activity of the relevant practitioner; the closer the correspondence the better. The student gains competence in an array of valued activities; he is thereby educated.

Advocates of "teaching about . . ." stress the *meaning* of an activity to the non-practitioner. The aim of the curriculum is to bring the student to comprehend the place of science in the general culture and economy; to understand the function of language and the effects of variations in linguistic usage; to critically appreciate works of art; to consider man as sapient and to understand the reason and unreason in his own life. Students are to be reflective; the curriculum aims to broaden and enrich their reflections. The assessment of the students' reflectiveness considers their ability to relate an activity to others and to consider an activity and its products from varied points of view: What is the economic value of science? What are the social sources and consequences of a piece of literature? How do the artist and the philosopher differ in their approaches to their subject matter? The student learns to elaborate meanings; he is thereby educated.

Of course, neither approach to curriculum is adequate. The two approaches, and the two aims, complement one another. "Teaching . . ." unduly emphasizes the productive aspects of human behavior; its orientation is analytic; its spirit conservative. "Teaching . . ." can provide the vividness, detail, and rigor of a specialized activity. "Teaching about . . ." unduly emphasizes the critical aspects of human behavior; its orientation is synthetic; its spirit is creative. "Teaching about . . ." can provide the comprehensiveness and adventure of an undefined exploration. A capacity acquired without an understanding of the possible consequences of its exercise is dangerous. An appreciation of the consequences of an activity without a reasonable sense of the content of the activity is vacuous. "Teaching . . ." and "teaching about . . ." must clearly be joined.

The practical joining of the two aims is no simple task. The competent critic and competent practitioner of an activity are rarely the same person. Thus a curriculum project must typically rely on different groups of individuals if it is to develop materials for both "teaching . . ." and for "teaching about . . .", and both groups must be given effective voice in curriculum decisions. This is, perhaps, most likely to happen when the project director is, himself, thoroughly schooled in the activity and also interested in the meaning of the activity in the broad course of human affairs.

FOURTEEN

ROBERT G. HANVEY

"CURRICULUM" AND THE CULTURE OF THE SCHOOLS

There is a science fiction story that tells of a man who died but, not knowing he was dead, continued to act as if still alive until, unbelieving, he was seized and cremated. This may be a fair depiction of the biological status of the schools. They are animated and will remain so for decades to come, partly because they serve important non-educational functions, but they may in fact be dead or dying, unable to respond effectively to the living environment.

I saw an administrative memo recently, written by an assistant superintendent. The memo called for changes in the local schools. But it went like this: "We ought to do x — but we can't because the parents would never allow it. We ought to do y — but the laws of the state do not permit. We ought to do z — but the teachers would protest." These caveats cannot be dismissed as mere rationalizations; they testify to the crystallized latticework of considerations and interests that makes the system so unyielding. *System,* of course, is the key word.

The reformers keep trying and, being almost uneducable, continue to be amazed at the slightness of effects wrought by their efforts. But each of them plays with pieces of the system and the pieces persist in springing back into original position.

The problem lies in our categories and in the differentiation of roles associated with the categories. The category "curriculum," to be bluntly specific, is not useful. It fosters tunnel vision and blinds the "curriculum theorist" or the "curriculum specialist" to most of the factors that bear on the educational experience. It connotes a specialized attention to the substance and sequence of courses, as if this can really be separated from questions of tenure, or grading systems, or student grouping, or room acoustics, or administrator style, or intellectual norms within the faculty.

At the moment, no one is backing off and looking at school as a total cultural system, at the ways in which the elements articulate and bear upon one another. The modular scheduling movement gave some promise in this direction, but important components of the traditional system — teacher work load and low expectations for teacher intellectualism — were not changed.

We need some mirrors, full-length ones, so that schools can see themselves whole. In the last few years the students have supplied the best mirrors, and in them we have seen tyrannies and irrelevancies which most educators, reformers among them, have taken for granted. What business was it of the curriculum innovators if school administrators chose to defend the American way of life by dictating length of hair and length of skirts? And weren't hall passes and hall guards a natural part of school life?

In the students' mirrors there are villains; in reality there are no villains. We are all victims of large-scale organization, of the specialization that comes with largeness, of the blindness that comes with specialized preoccupations. And, blindly, we try to adapt to the problems of large organizations by creating new specialized roles.

We might try smaller organizations, but we won't. We might try to discover if some important things are more effectively learned in non-school contexts, but that would hurt. We might publicly support some radical alternatives to school and let young people choose, but that would really hurt.

What we will do is continue to "reform." And the animal we call "school" will continue to breathe and to act, programmed by its own structure and quite unaffected by the nudges along its flanks.

ABOUT THE AUTHORS

EDWARD G. BEGLE is Professor of Education and Mathematics at Stanford University. As Director of SMSG, Professor Begle has had wide experience in problems of curriculum development in the field of mathematics education. In 1969, he was awarded the Award for Distinguished Service from the American Mathematical Association.

BENJAMIN S. BLOOM is the Charles H. Swift Distinguished Service Professor of Education at the University of Chicago. Professor Bloom specializes in the field of curriculum evaluation and is the author of several books in the field of education, including *Stability and Change in Human Characteristics,* and the editor of *Taxonomy of Educational Objectives: The Cognitive Domain.*

ROBERT G. BRIDGHAM is Assistant Professor of Education at Stanford University. His major interests lie in the study of the acquisition of scientific concepts by children. Professor Bridgham received his Ph.D. from Harvard University.

LEE J. CRONBACH is the Vida Jacks Professor of Education at Stanford University. His major interests lie in the area of educational measurement and educational psychology. Professor Cronbach is the author of *Essentials of Psychological Testing* and *Educational Psychology.*

ELLIOT W. EISNER is Professor of Education and Art at Stanford University. His major interests are in the area of curriculum theory and art education. In 1967, Professor Eisner was awarded the Palmer O. Johnson Memorial Award from the American Educational Research Association and in 1969 he received a Fellowship from the John Simon Guggenheim Foundation.

EDMUND BURKE FELDMAN is Professor of Art at the University of Georgia in Athens, Georgia. Professor Feldman's major interests are in the areas of art education and art criticism. He is the author of *Art as Image and Idea.*

Robert G. Hanvey was formerly a Project Director for the American Anthropological Association's Anthropology Study Project. He is now Associate Professor of Education at Indiana University. Prior to his work with the American Anthropological Association, he taught the social studies in the University High School at the University of Chicago.

Robert Karplus is Professor of Physics at the University of California, Berkeley. He is Director of the Science Curriculum Improvement Study, which is being used in elementary schools throughout the country.

Irving Kaufman was formerly Project Director in Art Education at the CAREL Educational Laboratory in Washington, D. C. He is now Associate Professor of Art at The City University of New York. Professor Kaufman is an exhibiting painter and has published poetry in journals in this country and abroad.

James B. Macdonald is Professor of Education at The University of Wisconsin, Milwaukee. He served as Visiting Professor in the Institute of Education at the University of London and has had a long-standing interest in the study of curriculum theory.

Richard E. Schutz is Director of the Southwest Regional Laboratory in Los Angeles, California. The program of the Laboratory includes projects of curriculum development in a wide range of subject matters. Prior to directing the Laboratory, Dr. Schutz was Professor of Education at the Arizona State University.

Michael Scriven is Professor of Philosophy at the University of California, Berkeley. His most widely known contributions to education are in the area of curriculum evaluation, especially the conceptualization of strategies for formative and summative evaluation.

Jan L. Tucker is Assistant Professor of Education at Stanford University. His major interests lie in the study of policy questions in the social studies. Professor Tucker received his Ph.D. from Indiana University.

Merlin C. Wittrock is Professor of Educational Psychology at the University of California, Los Angeles. Professor Wittrock was appointed a Fellow at the Center for Advanced Study in the Behavioral Sciences. His major interests are in the study of language learning.